Courtroom Interpreting

Marianne Mason

UNIVERSITY PRESS OF AMERICA,® INC.
Lanham • Boulder • New York • Toronto • Plymouth, UK

Copyright © 2008 by
University Press of America,® Inc.
4501 Forbes Boulevard
Suite 200
Lanham, Maryland 20706
UPA Acquisitions Department (301) 459-3366

Estover Road
Plymouth PL6 7PY
United Kingdom

Library of Congress Control Number: 2008926476
ISBN-13: 978-0-7618-4073-2 (paperback : alk. paper)
ISBN-10: 0-7618-4073-7 (paperback : alk. paper)
eISBN-13: 978-0-7618-4174-6
eISBN-10: 0-7618-4174-1

$\otimes^{\text{TM}}$ The paper used in this publication meets the minimum
requirements of American National Standard for Information
Sciences—Permanence of Paper for Printed Library Materials,
ANSI Z39.48—1992

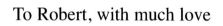
To Robert, with much love

Contents

Tables

Foreword

Courtroom Interpreting represents a useful contribution to the field of interpreting studies. Focusing on the setting of the courtroom, and in particular on witness testimony, Marianne Mason picks up where other scholars in the field of court interpreting have left off (Berk-Seligson 2002, Hale 2004, Mikkelson 1998, Rigney 1997, and Wadensjo 1992). Essentially, the research presented here provides further evidence of the challenges that court interpreters face, challenges of a cognitive sort. It demonstrates convincingly that cognitive overload will have an adverse effect on interpreter performance. Whereas much of previous empirical research in this field has been ethnographic in approach, and most scholars have looked at their data from the perspective of discourse analysis and linguistic pragmatics, *Courtroom Interpreting* looks at interpreted discourse from a psycholinguistic standpoint as well, taking into account the factor of memory and its relationship to interpreting quality.

Mason examines the relationship between utterance length and interpreters' treatment of style, syntax, meaning and intent. Utterance length is measured in relation to error rate along these different dimensions. Mason uncovers interpreter strategies for dealing with excessively long utterances: interrupting the witness and switching from consecutive to semiconsecutive interpreting. Each of these is analyzed with an eye on its impact on interpreting error rates. What sorts of pragmatic units are affected in the rendition of source language into target language are an important finding of this study. The author examines such linguistic variables as politeness markers, forms of address, grammatical case, pragmatic focus, lexicon, speech disfluencies (hesitations, repetitions), and discourse markers. Each of these is analyzed in its relation to length of turn.

The data set is rich: two-hundred hours of digitally recorded courtroom proceedings, randomly selected, in which twelve interpreters are heard in action. With a nearly equal distribution of men and women comprising the sample, the study notes differences in interpreting performance according to interpreter gender. Specifically, the study shows, women treat politeness markers and other forms of deference differently than do men when they are cognitively overloaded: they tend to omit them from their interpretations. Mason accounts for this finding with a sociolinguistic explanation, drawing on prior language and gender studies.

Courtroom Interpreting will be useful for those who train interpreters and for those who teach interpreting/translating courses at the undergraduate or post-baccalaureate level. It adds to the growing body of much needed empirically-oriented research on court interpreting.

Susan Berk-Seligson
Vanderbilt University
December, 2007

Preface

The linguistic study of courtroom interpreting has received a great deal of attention since the passing of the Court Interpreters Act of 1978. A comprehensive assessment of how well linguistic minorities are served by the judicial system is presented in Susan Berk-Seligson's (2002) seminal work *The Bilingual Courtroom*. In this work, Berk-Seligson applies the findings of prior research on language and the law (Lind and O'Barr 1979; O'Barr and Atkins 1980; O'Barr 1982) to the study of the Spanish/English bilingual courtroom. She finds that interpreters systematically change the style, tone, and content of the original. These changes can have a significant effect on jurors' impressions of witnesses and, possibly, on the outcome of a trial. Berk-Seligson's findings gave researchers in the field of forensic linguistics a vision of what could go wrong when linguistic minorities require the services of interpreters in the courtroom. This unprecedented view of the bilingual courtroom changed how many of us approach the study of courtroom interpreting and gave way to new research in the field (Edward 1995; Hale 2004; Rigney 1997). Much of this research focuses on describing the discourse features of courtroom interpreting. This approach provides a comprehensive description of the role of legal interpreters in the courtroom. The question that has remained unanswered is why do interpreters add to and omit from the original linguistic content?

The explanations for the interpreters' behavior in the courtroom seem to lie in both linguistic and cognitive factors. It is well established that interpreters who employ the consecutive mode of interpreting are often affected by cognitive overload (Gile 1995; Seleskovitch 1978). In this mode of interpreting, interpreters must remember a great deal of linguistic content while also observing the semantic, stylistic, and syntactic properties of the original. Court interpreters must accomplish this task with very little, if any, pre-trial preparation while contending with stress and fatigue (Moser-Mercer et al 1998; Vidal 1997).

This book seeks to provide the reader with cognitive and linguistic explanations for the interpreters' deviations from the source-language discourse. To my knowledge there is no single source that provides a comprehensive explanation for the linguistic behavior of courtroom interpreters. In the pages to follow, I will show how a cognitive analysis of the bilingual courtroom, coupled with the use of empirical testing, provide answers to many of the fundamental questions in courtroom interpreting research.

I hope this book offers a new direction for the study of courtroom interpreting. The field of courtroom interpreting would benefit from a new perspective that sheds light on the linguistic and cognitive challenges that court interpreters face every day when they take an oath to perform a faithful and accurate rendition of the original.

Marianne Mason
Georgia Institute of Technology
December, 2007

Acknowledgments

I would like to thank Ms. Patti Belcher, acquisitions editor, and the staff at the University Press of America for their assistance in getting this book published.

I would also like to thank the following people for their support in completing this book: Dr. Susan Berk-Seligson, Associate Professor of Spanish and Associate Director for Graduate Studies, Center for Latin American and Iberian Studies at Vanderbilt University, for having agreed so graciously to write the foreword for this book; Ms. Janis Palma, court certified interpreter and staff interpreter at the United States District Court for the district of Puerto Rico, for her insights into the bilingual courtroom and for her continuous support; Dr. Luis Mariano Negrón-Portillo, dean of the Interamerican University Law School, for having answered, at different points in the research phase of this book, questions about the inner workings of the legal system; and Leonard S. Rosenbaum for his indexing and proofreading services.

Finally, I would like to acknowledge my colleagues at the School of Modern Languages at the Georgia Institute of Technology for their words of encouragement, my students for all their best wishes, my family for their endless support and insightful comments and suggestions, and the staff at the federal district court house from which I obtained the data, in particular the chief justice, the clerk of the court, and the deputy court recorders and staff interpreters whose assistance was instrumental in the completion of this research (you know who you are!).

Chapter One

Introduction

A non-English speaking defendant requires the services of a court interpreter to receive a fair trial. The presence of a courtroom interpreter at trial, however, does not guarantee that a witness's "voice" will be captured faithfully in the interpreter's renditions. The interpreter may alter the style, structure, and/or intent of the witness's testimony, which may interfere with the defendant's constitutional right to a fair trial. Although there have been many explanations for the interpreter's treatment of the source-language discourse in the courtroom, none of these has provided a comprehensive view of the role that cognitive overload plays in the court interpreting process. Cognitive overload refers to the burden that a large amount of input places on the interpreter's memory and language processing ability. In this book, I will examine the relationship between memory load and the interpreter's performance. I will argue that without a more cognitive-based approach to the practice and training of courtroom interpreters, important information contained in the witness's "voice" will be lost, which could infringe on the rights of those who do not speak the language of the courts.

THE LEGAL HISTORY OF COURTROOM INTERPRETING IN THE UNITED STATES: ADDRESSING A HUMAN-RIGHTS ISSUE

The Constitution of the United States of America does not guarantee directly the right to an interpreter. Still denying a linguistic minority the right to an interpreter interferes with his or her constitutional right to a fair trail. The right to a fair trial in the United States extends to non-English-speaking defendants, and it is protected under the Fifth, Sixth, and Fourteenth Amendments.

The Fifth Amendment stipulates that an individual cannot be compelled to testify against him, or herself, in a criminal trial, nor be deprived of life, liberty, or property without due process of law. The Sixth Amendment adds that in criminal prosecutions the accused will be informed of the nature and cause of the accusation and will have the right to be confronted with the witnesses against him or her, as well as have the right to counsel in his or her defense. The rights stated under the Sixth Amendment imply that for a defendant to be able to assist in his or her own defense he or she needs to be able to communicate with counsel and provide counsel with informed input. If the defendant does not understand or speak the language of the court, he or she will require the assistance of an interpreter to secure his or her right to a fair trail. The Fourteenth Amendment extends the application of the Fifth and Sixth Amendments to all persons born or naturalized in the United States. This amendment asserts that no state can make or enforce any law that is aimed at depriving any person, within the state's jurisdiction, equal protection under the law. Under this amendment, all individuals whose cases are viewed in federal or state courthouses in the United States have the constitutional right to a fair trial, which for many linguistic minorities entails having the right to an interpreter.

Despite the presence and applicability of these amendments to the United States court system, a defendant's right to a fair trial and equal protection under the law has not been observed in all instances. The case of U.S. ex rel Negrón *v.* N.Y.,[1] for example, is one of the most significant cases in which a defendant's constitutional rights were violated because the services of a court interpreter were not provided. The case involved Rogelio Nieves-Negrón, a Puerto Rican farm laborer in Suffolk County, NY, who emigrated from Arecibo, Puerto Rico to the United States sometime between 1963 and 1965 to work as a potato packer. On the afternoon of August 10, 1966, Negrón killed Juan Del Valle, a fellow co-worker, in a drunken brawl. Negrón was subsequently arrested and charged with murder.

During the course of the trial, neither Negrón nor his attorneys requested the services of an interpreter. There was no communication between counsel and defendant, and in only a few instances an interpreter employed by the prosecution provided a summary translation into Spanish for Negrón. He was convicted of second-degree murder after a jury trial and was sentenced to twenty years to life imprisonment on March 10, 1967. As a result of the ruling, and after exhausting opportunities for direct review, Negrón's counsel filed an application for a *writ* of *habeas corpus* in the Eastern District of New York on June 25, 1969. Judge Bartels, who oversaw the case, granted Negrón his release subject to the state's prerogative to appeal or retry Negrón within thirty days. Judge Bartels' opinion,[2] as it regards Negrón's right to due process, reads as follows:

The Government contends that assuming Negron was entitled to a court appointed [*1309] interpreter, both he and his attorney waived this right by failing to request such an interpreter. To warrant the finding of waiver it must be clearly established that there was an intentional relinquishment or abandonment of a known right or privilege . . . In so doing, the court must "indulge every reasonable presumption against the waiver of fundamental constitutional rights" and "must be mindful at all times of the background, experience and general conduct of the accused alleged to have waived the right."

The government appealed Judge Bartel's ruling, but it was affirmed by the United States Court of Appeals for the Second Circuit. The judge in the case, Judge Kauffman, expanded on the previous ruling with the following opinion:[3]

It is axiomatic that the Sixth Amendment's guarantee of a right to be confronted with adverse witnesses, now also applicable to the states through the Fourteenth Amendment . . . includes the right to cross-examine those witnesses as an "an essential and fundamental requirement for the kind of fair trial which is this country's constitutional goal" . . . But the right that was denied Negrón seems to us even more consequential than the right of confrontation. Considerations of fairness, the integrity of the fact-finding process, and the potency of our adversary system of justice forbid that the state should prosecute a defendant who is not present at his own trial.

Judge Kauffman added that the government's claim that Negrón waived the right to an interpreter is unsound. He ruled that it would be erroneous to assume that the silence of Negrón and his counsel was part of counsel's strategy to secure a reversal of the prior ruling on appeal. The judge noted that he would be reluctant "to find a knowing, intelligent waiver of so ill-defined a right."

At the time the United States Court of Appeals for the Second Circuit viewed Negrón's case, the argument as to whether individuals have a right to a state provided interpreter was far from settled. As Pousada (1979:187) notes "the tendency in the past has been for the courts not to supply interpreters as a matter of course, and when interpreters have been appointed, it has been primarily for the convenience of the court, not the protection of the non-English-speaking party" The manner in which the United States court system treated non-English speakers, however, changed with the enactment of the Court Interpreters Act of 1978.[4]

THE ENACTMENT OF THE
COURT INTERPRETERS ACT OF 1978

The outcome of Negrón's case coupled with "the callousness with which the non-English speaker has been treated" (Pousada 1979:186) prompted advocates of linguistic minorities' rights to call for equal access to due process. Their calls led to the enactment of the Court Interpreters Act of 1978, which was later amended in 1988. This Act establishes a certification procedure for court interpreters and specifies the conditions under which the services of a court interpreter may be utilized. These conditions include that the witness or defendant speaks only or primarily a language other than the English language.

Since the enactment of the Court Interpreters Act of 1978, more than 30 states[5] have passed legislation that mandates the presence of interpreters in cases in which defendants or witnesses have minimal English skills. California, for example, is one of those states that have made provisions in its Constitution requiring a qualified interpreter in any criminal case in which a defendant does not speak English (Mikkelson, 1998:29).

Current legislation to protect the rights of linguistic minorities in the United States, however, has not erased entirely the many problems that non-English speakers may face in the United States judicial system. Benmaman (2000:2) warns that "we must not lose sight of the fact that the trial court has wide discretion in determining whether an interpreter is necessary for a defendant." The author explains that it is entirely within the trial courts discretion to determine who is qualified to serve as an interpreter. In addition, Benmaman points out that every state court also exercises the right to determine whether a defendant needs an interpreter, and only if a defendant has been deprived of a constitutional right, is it considered an abuse of the power of the courts.

In light of Benmaman's comments and the increased demand for court interpreters in Federal District Courts, one can only expect that the concerns surrounding the appointment of court interpreters in federal courts will continue and become more widespread. The latter warrants further evaluation given current population trends in the United States.

The Census of 2000 reports that the Hispanic population in the United States has reached the 38.8 million mark and projects that the Hispanic population is likely to continue to grow. In 2004, this population group accounted for over 50% of the total growth in population in the United States. Of the Hispanics surveyed in the Census of 2000, 71% believe that they speak English either well or very well. Twenty-eight percent, however, believe that they do not speak English well or that they do not speak English at all. This number accounts for a significant percentage of the Hispanic population, some of which may require the assistance of a court interpreter in their lifetime.

The growing trend in the Hispanic population correlates with the increased number of interpreting events in the United States courts. For example, the Administrative Office of the United States Courts reports that in 2005 the District courts used interpreters in 227,461 events, which is a 1.5% increase[6] from the year before. Of all of the languages[7] used in the United States District Courts, Spanish is the most commonly used language for interpreters and accounts for 94% (214,355) of all reported interpreting events. These numbers should not surprise us, because Spanish speakers account for the largest non-English-speaking group in the United States. Moreover, they account for the majority of illegal[8] immigrants crossing the United States border and potentially needing the services of an interpreter.

The current and projected statistics from the United States Census and the Administrative Office of the U.S. Courts, coupled with the significance of landmark cases, make it essential that we understand fully the manner in which courtroom interpreters are expected to protect the legal rights of non-English speaking minorities.

THE RESPONSIBILITIES OF THE LEGAL INTERPRETER

The National Association of Judicial Interpreters (NAJIT) Code of Ethics and Professional Responsibilities provides guidelines[9] that an interpreter must observe when carrying out his or her responsibilities in the courtroom. These guidelines specify that courtroom interpreters must render the source-language speech faithfully into the target language. This includes the rendition of all linguistic content that provides style and tone to the original, such as hedges, false starts, and repetitions.

In studies conducted by Berk-Seligson (1987, 2002), Hale (1995, 2004), and Rigney (1997) that examine the interpreter's actual, rather than expected, behavior in the courtroom, interpreters often did not follow their professional code. Berk-Seligson, for example, finds that interpreters systematically add and omit those linguistic elements that assign style and tone to the original. Hale also finds evidence of the interpreters' mistranslation of pragmatic content. She mentions that "despite common belief that legal terminology is the biggest obstacle for court interpreters, what proved most difficult for them was achieving equivalence at the pragmatic level" (1995:205).

Both Berk-Seligson and Hale suggest that interpreters may alter the testimony style of the original, because interpreters do not consider pragmatic content to be salient enough. Rigney (1997) also finds that interpreters alter the style and tone of the original, but Rigney provides a different explanation for this linguistic outcome. She argues that court interpreters often disregard a variety of discourse markers (*DM*) primarily because of structural needs and processing difficulty:

> Discourse marker use, in general, seems to be dispreferred and avoided even though in those cases where it should be expected (i.e. 'literal interpretation' in the sense of complete and as close to the original as possible, as it is required in

the courtroom). But when DM are interpreted in the courtroom, the interpretation of DM seems to be conditioned by several factors which respond to criteria
of equivalence in both languages . . . structural needs and processing difficulties
(1995:127).

Although the explanations for the interpreter's systematic alteration of the
linguistic content of the original are varied, the solutions put forth to address
this issue often led researchers to the same conclusion—courtroom interpreters need to be better trained.

Berk-Seligson (2002:204), for example, notes that if interpreters are not
qualified to perform their duties in the courtroom, "the product of their efforts
is bound to be faulty." She argues that it would be naïve for a judge to expect
that swearing in an interpreter will guarantee an accurate translation of courtroom proceedings, even if the interpreter is not well trained and competent.

One of the solutions that have been put forth to remedy interpreters' linguistic intrusiveness in the courtroom stresses the need for specialized training and effective certification programs.[10] The Director of the Administrative
Office of the United States Courts prescribes, determines, and certifies the
qualifications of those who may serve as certified interpreters. Federal certification is given to those interpreters who have passed the Federal Court Interpreters Examination, which is a test constructed and administered by the
Administrative Office of the United States Courts.

The Federal Court Interpreters Examination consists of two sections: a
written and an oral examination. The written component consists of multiple-
choice tests: one in English and one in Spanish. Once the candidate passes
both the English and Spanish written components of the examination, he or
she may take the oral component. The oral examination tests the candidate's
knowledge of legal terminology and interpreting skills. It also tests three
types of interpreting styles: consecutive, simultaneous, and sight translation.

From these types of interpreting styles, consecutive interpreting allows the
interpreter to start his or her rendition once the speaker completely finishes
his or her speech, whereas in simultaneous interpreting the interpreter listens
and speaks at the same time. Sight interpreting or sight translation, as it is also
known, combines both interpreting and translation tasks, and it is used when
an interpreter reads a written document in the source language and translates
it orally into the target language.

In fiscal year 2005, the Administrative Office of the United States Courts
reported that of 367 examinees who took the oral examination, 81 (22%)
passed the two-part examination and are now federally certified court interpreters. Since the certification process began in 1980, 1,032 interpreters have
been certified. The low number of candidates who pass both the written and

oral parts of the examination reflects, in part, the difficulty of the test. The main purpose of this test is to ensure that only the most qualified of interpreters become certified and are allowed to work in the courts.

A benefit of creating rigorous standards for courtroom interpreters, specifically the requirement that they be certified when working in the federal court system, is that it may help ensure that the interpreter's renditions reflect the linguistic properties of the original. Although there is legal precedence[11] that defendants don't have a constitutional right to a flawless translation, commentators suggest that "interpreters should strive to translate exactly what is said and should not 'embellish' or 'summarize' live testimony" (Benmaman, 2000:10). In the works of Berk-Seligson (2002) and Hale (2004), the importance of abiding to this standard is shown. The authors demonstrate that an interpreter's rendition can change the linguistic qualities of the original testimony, which can potentially shape how a jury perceives a witness and, thus, affect the outcome of a trial.

COGNITIVE FACTORS: THE CONFLICT BETWEEN THE ABILITIES AND RESPONSIBILITIES OF A COURTROOM INTERPRETER

There is a large gap between what is expected of a court interpreter and what actually occurs in the bilingual courtroom. Although interpreters are expected to function in an unobtrusive manner, almost as machines, the reality is that the quality of an interpreter's renditions is affected by cognitive, environmental, and competency factors.

Although recent studies (Berk-Seligson 2002; Hale 2004) have served to increase awareness of the difficulties interpreters face when performing their duties in the courtroom, court interpreters still continue to be the "Cinderella" (Repa 1991:595) of the interpreting profession. As Morris (1995) notes, many in the legal profession believe that interpreters should provide a literal rendition of courtroom proceedings:

> When rendering meaning from one language to another, court interpreters are not to interpret—this being an activity which only lawyers are to perform, but to translate—a term which is defined, sometimes expressively and sometimes by implication, as rendering the speaker's words verbatim. (31).

A focus on form, particularly on semantic content, can tax the interpreter's memory unnecessarily and result in erroneous translations (Seleskovitch 1975). Court interpreters, thus, are often advised to mediate between providing a rendition that focuses on conceptual units while also maintaining the style of the original:

> This so-called "verbatim requirement" is a source of confusion to many, because it is assumed to mean that a word-for-word or literal translation is required . . . What is really required is that the interpreter account for every word and every other element of meaning in the source-language message. Thus, if a witness answers the source-language equivalent of, "I, well, I don't know . . . I suppose . . . yes, I think I saw him there", the interpreter's version in English should not simply be "I think I saw him there," but should reflect all of the uncertainty conveyed in the original (Mikkelson 1999:1).

The rationale for maintaining style, tone, and intent in the bilingual courtroom is a sound one. As Gonzáles, Vázquez, and Mikkelson (1991) explain, "the goal of a court interpreter is to enable the judge and jury to react in the same manner to a non-English-speaking witness as they do with one who speaks English" (17). This requires, however, that the interpreter place a great deal of listening and processing effort on recalling precise stylistic and extralinguistic content.

The interpreter must be able to maintain the tone and register of the original while also providing a faithful rendition of the syntactic structure and semantic content of the source language. The work of court interpreters, thus, puts unique demands on their linguistic and cognitive abilities. A failure to capture the stylistic, syntactic, and semantic content of the original may alter the outcome of a courtroom proceeding (Berk-Seligson 2002).

In addition to the linguistic expectations that court interpreters must fulfill, they must also contend with stress, fatigue (Moser-Mercer et al. 1998; Vidal 1997), and cognitive factors that affect the interpreters' processing capacity greatly. Courtroom interpreters, for example, unlike conference interpreters (Niska 1995), rarely work in teams and are expected to work without prior preparation or knowledge of the case. As Mikkelson (1999:6) notes, "the interpreter is not given a script in this production, however, he is expected to improvise while other players act out previously rehearsed parts."

Interpreters are expected also to work for long stretches of time without taking any breaks. Researchers have found that the effects of fatigue on the quality of an interpreter's renditions are significant. Moser-Mercer and her colleagues (1998) suggest that frequency of errors, particularly meaning-based errors, rise steadily as the interpreters get closer to 30 minutes on the job. In the authors' study, the error rate rose even further once the interpreters reached the 60-minute mark. Their results indicate that all subjects combined committed an average of 32.5 meaning-based errors per unit of time tested. The authors state that "considering that each meaning error, no matter how minor, does distort the message, a considerable increase in the number of meaning errors after 30 minutes on task does represent a significant decline in output" (1998:56).

The researchers' findings are important for this book because fatigue, as the variable turn length, affects the interpreter's processing capacity. In consecutive court interpreting, interpreters face long intervals between receiving input and producing output. An important portion of the input, for example, provides stylistic and extralinguistic information that the interpreter is expected to recall in a fairly literal fashion. The requirement to provide all stylistic and extralinguistic content, coupled with the pressure interpreters feel to maintain syntactic and semantic equivalence, taxes the interpreters' cognitive processes and is often unattainable at increasing turn length.

The degree to which turn length affects the interpreter's ability to maintain linguistic equivalence in his or her renditions can be estimated statistically by examining the relationship between interpreter-induced errors and turn length. The results of this analysis will provide a measurement of the size of the problem and may be used to direct the training efforts of courtroom interpreters toward more cognitive-based approaches, such as the use of semiconsecutive interpreting and the note-taking technique.

THE PURPOSE AND GOALS OF THE STUDY

The main goal of this book is to examine the direct effects of cognitive overload on courtroom interpreting. In this research, cognitive overload is measured as the effect of turn length or volume (Palma 1995:219) on the interpreters' renditions. In courtroom interpreting, interpreters are expected to provide a faithful rendition of all semantic, syntactic, and pragmatic content regardless of the length of an utterance. This expectation carries a cost that needs to be addressed if the quality of the interpreters' renditions is to improve.

In this book, I will show that as the length of an utterance increases and the interpreter is expected to recall more linguistic and pragmatic information, the rate of interpreter-induced errors rises significantly. These errors, which have not been quantified prior to this study, are most often those that alter the stylistic qualities of the original. These types of errors have been shown to potentially affect jurors' impression of witnesses and the outcome of a trial (Berk-Seligson 2002).

The secondary goal of this book is to examine the strategies that court interpreters use, and could use, to restrict the effect that turn length has on the quality of their renditions. In addition, I will examine whether the types of errors interpreters make are related to their gender. Quantifying the data by gender, which to my knowledge has not been previously researched, will provide some insights into the possible gender differences in managing cognitive overload. Gender differences, if found, would need to be accounted for in the training of courtroom interpreters and in the design of future research.

In sum, the relevance of this research is that it provides researchers and courtroom interpreters an estimate of the magnitude of the burden that turn length imposes on the interpreter. These findings may serve to direct the efforts of those who work on the research, legal, and training side of courtroom interpreting. From a research perspective, this study could be used for its methodological and data-analysis contributions. From a legal perspective, the results of this study could provide evidence of the need to stop seeing the courtroom interpreter as an invisible, and detached, part of courtroom proceedings. The working conditions of court interpreters and their performance cannot improve unless the court system recognizes the effect that the requirement for "accuracy," particularly at higher turn lengths, has on memory load and on the quality of the interpreter's renditions. From a training perspective, the results of this study may direct the interpreter's efforts at focusing more aggressively on strategies that reduce cognitive overload, as those observed in other venues that use consecutive interpreting, such as conference interpreting (Gile 1990; Dollerup and Loddegaard 1992).

OVERVIEW OF CHAPTERS

The introduction of this book provides the reader with an overview of the interpreter's role and responsibilities in the bilingual courtroom, specifically the Spanish/English courtroom. Chapter 2 describes the fieldwork procedures that were used to obtain and to study the data. Chapter 3 provides a detailed account of the relationship between turn length and the interpreters' additions, omissions, and changes. This chapter will examine and quantify the effect of the interpreters' renditions on the style, meaning, and intent of the original utterance. The statistical portion of this study will consist of a regression analysis. This type of analysis has many advantages over a correlation analysis or a difference in means test. It allows for the simultaneous testing of multiple linguistic variables and accounts for the portion of the error terms that are explained by the relationship of the linguistic variables under observation.

Chapter 4 examines two strategies that interpreters use to deal with the high demands that the interpreting process places on their memory: the interpreters' interruption of a witness and use of the semiconsecutive mode. This chapter evaluates the uses, costs, and possible benefits of each strategy, whereas Chapter 5 draws analogies between the interpreters' use of length-reducing strategies, specifically the semiconsecutive mode and note-taking. The possible benefits of note-taking in courtroom interpreting, as well as the need for future study on its uses in the courtroom, will also be discussed. Chapter 6 considers whether the gender of an interpreter is significantly related to the number of errors observed in the data. This chapter will also evaluate whether the interpreter's gender is related to the types of additions and omissions observed in the courtroom. The gender factor may have significant implications in the training of courtroom interpreters. Lastly, Chapter 7 presents a summary and concluding comments about courtroom interpreting in light of the linguistic and statistical findings.

NOTES

1. Negrón v. State of New York, 310 F. Supp. 1304 (E.D.N.Y. 1970).

2. Judge Bartel's opinion included the citation of the following seminal cases: United States v. Drummond, *supra*, 354 F.2d at 148 and United States ex rel. Elksnis v. Gilligan, 2.56 F. Supp. 244 (S.D.N.Y. 1966).

3. United States Court of Appeals for the Second Circuit, 434 F. 2d 386; 1970. No. 112, Docket No. 34885.

4. See Appendix 1.

5. These states belong to the Consortium for State Court Interpreter Certification (see www.ncsconline.org).

6. Statistics from the Administrative Office of the United States Courts indicate that in 2004 there were 223,996 interpreting events in Federal District Courts.

7. In the fiscal year 2005, the languages that required the most interpreters in the United States District Courts, excluding Spanish, are: Mandarin (1,792), Portuguese (1,361), Arabic (1250), Vietnamese (863), Korean (796), Cantonese (745), Russian (610), French (417), and Foochow (409). These languages individually account for less than 1% of all interpreting events in 2005.

8. See "Court Interpreters Feel Impact of Illegal Immigration Caseload" Newsletter of the Federal Courts 37(2), 2005, <http://www.uscourts.gov/ttb/ feb05ttb/ interpreters/index.html> (5 Feb. 2006).

9. See Appendix 2.

10. Some of the most established interpreting programs in the United States are housed in the following institutions of higher education: The Monterrey Institute of International Studies (M.A. in Translation and Interpretation; M.A. in Conference Interpretation), Florida International University (Certificate in Legal Translation and Court Interpreting), the College of Charleston (M.A. in Bilingual Legal Interpreting; Certificate in Bilingual Legal Interpreting), and San Diego State University (Certificate in Court Interpreting).

11. See Benmanan (2000: 10) for a complete description of the following cases: U.S. v Gómez, 1990, FL CA 11(902 F2d 809), Spruance v State, 1994, Del Sup (LEXIS 106), Ohio v Sánchez, 1986, OH App (LEXIS 6536), Liu v State, 1993, Del

Sup (628 A2d 1376), State v Mora, 1993, RI (518 A2d 1275), State v Rodríguez, 1994 LA App, 4th Cir (835 So 2d 391), Rodríguez v State, 1999, Supreme Court of Georgia (WL 371629), Check v State, 1999, Ga App (WL 236291), Levario v Texas, 1999, Tex. App-Texarkana (WL 289239), New York v Staley, 1999, N.Y.App.Div (LEXIS 6536), U.S. v Mata, 1999 (4th Cir. Virginia), State v Pérez, 1999 (WL 157644), Kan v Texas, 1999, Tex, App San Antonio (WL 417827).

Chapter Two

A Journey into Courtroom Interpreting: Fieldwork Procedures

This chapter discusses the steps that were taken to collect a substantial amount of courtroom data that allowed the researcher to test the extent of the relationship between interpreter-induced errors and increased memory load. The search for the data and its subsequent collection was the first and most significant step for making connections between the linguistic, cognitive, and training aspects of courtroom interpreting.

FIELDWORK

Fieldwork for this study was conducted in the summer of 2005 in a First Circuit Federal District Courthouse, which is located in a large metropolitan area. This particular courthouse hears a large number of cases that require the use of interpreters to translate in the Spanish/English mode. This courthouse, thus, was an ideal setting from which to access court-interpreted data. The process of obtaining access to the human and technical resources of the court, however, was, at best, difficult. I found early in the planning stages of the research that courtroom data could be acquired only through the direct consent of the chief federal district court judge.

Even though court proceedings are open to the public, data from live courtroom proceedings are available through members of the court, such as deputy clerks, court reporters, and staff interpreters. Their main duty, as expected, is to serve the court and only with the approval of those who directly (clerk of the court) or indirectly (chief court judge) oversee the work of courtroom staff can the resources of the court be made accessible for research. In this study, the chief judge and the clerk of the court proved indispensable in gaining access to the courtroom's resources.

To complete this research at the federal district courthouse, I prepared a proposal that laid out my research objectives and presented it to the chief judge for his approval. The chief judge approved the research and gave me permission to talk to staff members and to access court-interpreted data from the courthouse's digital area network. At the chief judge's request, the clerk of the court, who supervises the work of all staff members, and the supervisory court interpreter coordinated the logistical aspects of the data-gathering process.

It would be fair to note that one of the conditions requested by the chief judge was not to reveal the location of the court, specific case numbers, or the identity of any of the parties included in the data, such as attorneys, judges, plaintiffs, defendants, and witnesses. As with any type of forensic data, confidentiality is necessary to preserve the integrity of the legal process and to guarantee the privacy of those involved in a legal proceeding. In this book, the identity of all individuals has been kept confidential. Only initials, for interpreter (I), attorney (A), and witness (W), are maintained in the research. Following the chief judge's directive, the physical location of the court and the names of cases reviewed in this study have also been kept confidential.

THE NATURE OF THE DATA

The courtrooms of the First Circuit Federal District Courthouse are equipped with state-of-the-art-evidence-presentations equipment. The courtrooms have audio and video capabilities, which allow for the recording of courtroom proceedings. Furthermore, the courtrooms are equipped with real-time technology, and courtroom proceedings are digitally recorded. Digital recordings are archived in the court's local area network, and CD-ROM copies are available on demand for members of the court for later transcript production.

The advances in technology that were available at the time of this research allowed me to avoid some of the problems and limitations noted in previous research (Berk-Seligson 2002). In the past, studies of this kind were hampered by a number of limitations, such as anticipating the occurrence of scheduled interpreted proceedings, obtaining data that include many hours of interpreted material, and capturing the speech of all parties in the courtroom clearly. These problems were not encountered in this study.

Data for this study was accessed with the assistance of three court reporters and two courtroom deputies. Because court reporters and deputy clerks keep detailed records of each case, they are able to determine whether a case includes an interpreter or includes many hours of linguistic material. The court reporters' assistance and the nature of the data made it possible for me to avoid the problems associated with anticipating a courtroom proceeding that required the services of an interpreter.

The courthouse in this study hears both criminal and civil cases. My preference, however, was to examine only civil cases. The decision to use civil cases was a practical one. These cases are lengthy and often include many hours of interpreted testimony. Most criminal procedures in the courthouse's database consist of arraignments, which proved too short to be of scientific or empirical use for this study. The linguistic material contained in an arraignment is often formulaic and does not deviate from a prescribed "script." The interpreters, hence, know beforehand what to "interpret" during an arraignment. This type of material is often rendered in what seems to be the simultaneous mode. This form of interpreting would not have been suitable for inclusion in this study, because there are few, if any, constraints on memory, and the effects of cognitive overload on the quality of the interpreter's renditions cannot be observed easily or quantified.

Another advantage of using digital recordings lies in their superior audio quality and reach. Because the courtrooms of the First Circuit Federal District Courthouse are wired for real-time technology, the speech of all parties was captured clearly. Real-time technology also captures all aspects of a courtroom proceeding. This includes the judge's sidebar comments, which, although not part of this study, provided insights into counsel's strategy and, on occasion, into the judge's feelings toward a case. There were very few instances in which the speech of any of the parties in the courtroom, in particular the interpreter's, was unintelligible.

At the end of the summer research period, 200 hours of digitally recorded courtroom proceedings had been acquired. The data was randomly selected. In this study convenience sampling or the selection of subjects based on their availability, or on the researcher's personal preferences, would have constituted a major weakness of this research (Gile 1994:48) and was purposely avoided.

THE INTERPRETERS

This study includes 12 interpreters, 7 female and 5 male, who were randomly selected. The interpreters are court certified as required by law.[1] Seven of the interpreters work as staff members of the court. Federal district courthouses, which are located in large metropolitan areas, such as Los Angeles, Miami, and New York, and which have a large Hispanic population, often employ full-time interpreters. The other five interpreters freelance and are not permanent staff members of the court. Freelancing is very common in the court interpreting profession, and in the United States it is often the norm.

Throughout the data-gathering stages, I had the opportunity to talk to the court's staff interpreters. I inquired about their working conditions, the techniques they use to improve their renditions and to reduce stress, and their attendance at training seminars. The interpreters all mentioned that stress, lack of time for pre-trial preparation, and high volume/density utterances are the main causes of fatigue in the courtroom. They noted that they work long hours, with very few breaks, and have little or no time to brief before a proceeding. The interpreters remarked that it is stressful to have to switch from a case that uses a great deal of medical jargon, such as a medical malpractice case, to a case that uses legal jargon. They also mentioned that it is difficult to deal with witnesses and/or attorneys who are verbose and who use lengthy utterances. This seems to be the case with many of the attorneys and expert witnesses in this study.

The interpreters' remarks about their working conditions prompted me to inquire on whether they felt that the court system and academics' impressions about their work had misrepresented their role in the courtroom. This question gathered the most emotional and animated responses. Many of the interpreters, although valued the findings of prior research, felt that the difficulties of their work were not given enough attention. They also mentioned that the view that many in the legal community have about their role in the courtroom, particularly of being invisible, is to a great extent true. The legal profession, in particular attorneys, very rarely considers the difficulties of the interpreting process when examining witnesses.

The next question that arose naturally from the interpreters' candid comments was whether they use any interpreting techniques to reduce the detrimental effect of environmental factors and cognitive overload such as note-taking and visualization techniques. The interpreters noted that although they do practice some memory-building techniques and work on building their vocabulary, they rarely take notes. They remarked that if they take notes, it is reserved mostly for names and figures. One of the interpreters who had worked over 20 years in multiple federal and state courthouses, and who was involved heavily in providing training seminars, said that less than 50% of court interpreters use note-taking. For some of the interpreters, the consensus was that note taking, though it has merits, takes too much time and reduces their ability to store large chunks of information into memory.

Many of the court interpreters I interviewed mentioned that they have often used the interrupting-the-witness technique. Interruptions were observed in the data and, as noted in prior studies (Berk-Seligson 2002; Mikkelson 1991), seem to be one of the preferred modes of addressing cognitive overload and stress in the courtroom. The interpreters explained that interrupting the witness, when needed, gave them control over the interpreting process, and to some extent, over the witness and/or attorney. In a setting, where interpreters feel that they have little control, the use of interruptions (although it may carry more costs than benefits) appears to be an attractive and effective choice.

THE TRANSCRIPTION OF THE DATA

I expected the transcription stage of the data to be lengthy because the data was 200 hours long. Although I would have been able to request certified transcripts from the court reporters for a fee, this option was not feasible. The court record only reflects the interpreter's rendition, which meant that I could not verify the accuracy of the translation. Furthermore, even if I could have obtained a complete transcript of the court proceedings that comprise my data, researchers (Blackwell 1996; Fraser 2003; Shuy 1998; Storey 1995, 1996) in forensic linguistics have found these to be notoriously unreliable and often riddled with errors. The latter makes the use of transcripts unsuitable for linguistic analysis.

Once I decided that the court-certified transcripts were not a reliable option, I opted to transcribe the entire data set, which put my linguistic skills to the test. Although I am fully bilingual in English and Spanish and have worked as a translator for many years, I knew the difficulties of performing the transcription of the data. Nonetheless, I was intent on securing the confidentiality of the speakers and wanted to have control over the quality of the process. To ensure the quality of the transcripts, I was mindful to avoid the negative consequences of transcribing for long intervals without taking frequent breaks. As expected, it took many months to finish the first draft of the transcript. The transcripts were revised on multiple occasions before a final version was selected for study.

The analysis of the final version of the data includes not only a qualitative and quantitative examination of the data but also the preparation of a translated and revised version of the interpreters' renditions. This translation is key to presenting and accounting for those instances in which the interpreter makes additions, omissions, or changes to the linguistic variables present in the original. The translated text, however, should not be used to judge the capacity or competence of the interpreters in this study. In fairness to those interpreters whose work comprises the data, the cognitive demands and working conditions of producing a translation are unlike those faced in courtroom interpreting. When performing a translation, written input is permanently available and, as such, it is not necessary to keep it in memory.

A NOTE ON TRANSCRIPT CONVENTIONS

In this book, I took great care to maintain consistency with the transcription conventions. For example, I observed that there seems to be great variability in the transcript conventions used by different authors. Some use very complex transcription conventions that include very detailed notes on a speaker's utterances, as for example a speaker clearing his or her throat or coughing. Other authors use simpler transcription conventions that include only linguistic information that is relevant to further the points discussed in their research. The conventions used in this book are simple and straightforward.

The transcript conventions used in this study include the following:

—	The end, and the beginning, of a repaired utterance, as for example: Witness: I was—I was
[*Italics*]	A word, or phrase, that is added, omitted, or changed in a translation.
__ __	The end of a turn of talk,[2] the onset of an interruption or semiconsecutive interpreting, and the resumption of a speaker's utterance:
	Witness: I was at the office—
	Interpreter: Estaba en la oficina—
	Witness: —Y escuche una discusión—
	Interpreter: And I heard an argument—
(Translation)	The researcher's translation of the content of a turn of talk or utterance
CAPITALS	The witness's or interpreter's use of loud speech

They are simple for ease of reading and comprehension. Simplicity, however, does not exclude a lack of relevant linguistic information. All linguistic variables, including pauses and self-repairs, are accounted for in the text as well as all additions, omissions, and changes.

NOTES

1. The Federal Court Interpreters Act of 1978 requires that interpreters who work in the Spanish/English mode in the United States federal court system demonstrate proficiency by passing a certification exam.

2. For the purpose of this analysis, the term *turn of talk* (Sacks et al. 1974) will be used to denote the attorney's questions and the witness's responses, which can range from minimal, such as "uh," to a number of sentences.

Chapter Three

A Linguistic and Cognitive View of Interpreter-Induced Errors

This chapter will examine the relationship between turn length and the interpreter's rendition of style, grammar, meaning, and intent. It will be argued that an understanding of the cognitive effects of turn length on the linguistic variables is needed to account for a significant portion of interpreters' additions, omissions, and changes. By incorporating the role of cognitive overload in the study of courtroom interpreting, it will be possible to make recommendations that may result in the overall improvement of interpreters' renditions. These results, thus, will have practical applications in the fields of law and interpreting. The implications for the legal community lie in limiting the influence that courtroom interpreters seem to exert on jurors. The implications for the interpreting community lie in providing interpreters with a clearer picture of the extent that cognitive factors, such as cognitive overload, affect the interpreting and legal process. As this chapter will demonstrate, to improve the quality of court interpreters' renditions, the training of courtroom interpreters must address more forcefully the detrimental effect that turn length has on interpreters' treatment of style, topic management, syntax, meaning, and intent.

TURN LENGTH AND INTERPRETER-INDUCED ERRORS

In this study, turn length is defined as the number of linguistic elements, not just words, in a turn of talk. These linguistic elements include content words, such as nouns and verbs, as well as extralinguistic features, such as speech disfluencies, and pragmatic markers. The choice to include all linguistic content in a turn of talk allows me to establish a statistical relationship between what is often expected of courtroom interpreters, that is, the *verbatim requirement*, and the quality of interpreters' renditions. The latter is judged on the presence or absence of interpreter-induced errors.

It is important to note that in this study the product of an interpreter's efforts is not judged based on his or her ability to perform a word-matching exercise, but rather on the manner in which interpreters maintain the stylistic and linguistic properties of the original. Research on language and the law (Berk-Seligson 2002; Edwards 1995; Hale 2004; González, Vázques, and Mikkelson 1991; Morris 1995; Rigney 1997) has identified an array of interpreter-induced errors in the form of additions, omissions, and changes that affect the quality of interpreters' efforts. In the next sections, I will discuss the linguistic variables that were found to contribute to stylistic and linguistic changes in the data.

Effect on Style

The source of many of the interpreters' deviations from the original can frequently be traced back to their treatment of linguistic markers. Interpreters, through their addition or omission of pragmatic markers, such as speech disfluencies and the marker "well," can change the style and register of the source language discourse. In ethnolinguistic studies, such as O'Barr's (1982), the presence or absence of stylistic markers in courtroom discourse is found to have significant legal implications in the manner in which mock jurors evaluated witnesses.

O'Barr is one of the first to study the effect that witnesses' use of *powerless* or, alternatively, *powerful* speech styles have on juror evaluations of witnesses. He defines *powerless speech* as a type of speech style that includes many of the linguistic features that are associated with Lakoff's (1975) research on women's speech, such as hedges, polite forms, and tag questions, as well as other linguistic features that are not, such as pauses and hesitations.

In his study, O'Barr recreates the testimony of an actual trial using actors and a mock jury. The original testimony was edited for the purposes of the experiment. A *powerless* style, which was close to the original, and a *powerful* style, which omits the speaker's use of discourse markers, hesitation forms, and intensifiers, were produced and recorded using actors. Ninety-six undergraduate students from the University of North Carolina, Chapel Hill listened to the recordings and served as mock jurors in the experiment. After the students listened to the recordings, they were given a questionnaire that asked about their reactions to the case and to the individuals involved. The information collected revealed that "jurors" found "witnesses" who used the *powerful* style more believable, convincing, and trustworthy than "witnesses" who gave their testimony in the *powerless* style, regardless of the "witness" gender.

The implications of O'Barr's findings inspired, to a great extent, Berk Selig-son's (2002) and Hale's (2004) ethnolinguistic analysis of the bilingual court-room. The authors find that interpreters often add and omit those linguistic markers that alter the stylistic qualities of the original. Berk-Seligson (2002), in particular, performs her own study with mock jurors and finds that interpreter's treatment of language style in the courtroom has an effect on jurors. She shares many findings with O'Barr (1982), particularly the effect of pauses and prag-matic markers on jurors' evaluation of a witness. However, her findings suggest that mock jurors form a positive impression of witnesses who use polite and hy-percorrect speech. This is contrary to O'Barr's findings, which indicate that ju-rors form negative impressions of witnesses who use these forms of speech.

In this study, I observed interpreters adding and, most often, omitting sty-listic variables, such as speech disfluencies, pragmatic markers, and polite-ness markers that affect the register and tone of the original. The focus of the discussion, however, is not on testing the impact of these features on mock jurors, I will assume that prior findings on the effect of speech styles in the courtroom hold, but rather on examining whether there is a relationship be-tween interpreters' treatment of language style and increasing turn length. In this study, turn length is considered a potential trigger for interpreters' addi-tion or omission of stylistic variables in the bilingual courtroom and, thus, will be quantified to determine the statistical significance of the relationship.

Speech Disfluencies

The speaker's response to uttering a less-than-felicitous turn is to hesitate, re-peat a word, and use expressions such as "um," "uh," or, "oh." This linguis-tic response is observed in spontaneous conversation, and it is present in all types of discourse (Brennan and Schober 2001; Levelt 1989).

Court interpreters may add or omit speech disfluencies, such as pauses and repetitions, from their renditions. The interpreters' omission of pause mark-ers, however, was the most commonly observed in the data:

(1) A: When you came out of the car, where you holding something in your hand?

I: ¿Cuando usted se bajó del carro llevaba algo en la mano?

W: *Eh, eh* no llevaba nada. Porque pongo las manos en el pavimento y no podía tener nada en las manos si iba a bajarme del vehículo para hacer lo que él me decía. (Uh, Uh. I didn't have anything. Because, I put my hands on the pavement and I couldn't have anything in my hands, if I was going to get out of the vehicle to do as he said.)

I: No. I didn't have anything in my hands, because I put my hands on the floor and I couldn't have anything in them as I was getting out of the ve-hicle to do what he told me to do.

This example shows how the witness expresses some initial hesitation when responding to the attorney's question. For example, the witness's use of pause markers may signal a reluctance to respond or the witness's struggle to find an appropriate answer. By omitting the pause marker, the interpreter removes the witness's hesitation. This results in a more upfront, and possibly credible, account of what transpired during the evening the witness was placed under arrest. This rendition is problematic because the witness is suing the police department and the municipality on the grounds that he was wrongfully arrested and was the victim of police brutality.

To understand the possible source of the omissions, I examined the location of the speech disfluencies in the turn and the length of the utterance. I find that most omissions occur at the onset of the utterance where most of the speech-disfluencies in the data are observed. Although not all onset-initial speech disfluencies are omitted in the data, those that are omitted are found, on average, at onset-initial position and in utterances that exceed nine words. What these observations seem to suggest is that less linguistic information may remain available for recall when it occurs at the onset of a lengthier turn of talk.

Powerless "Well"

The discourse marker "well" is another type of linguistic marker that is often added to or omitted from the interpreters' renditions. This topic marker, which is defined in the literature as a meaningless particle (Berk-Seligson 2002:180; O'Barr 1982:67), can take a variety of pragmatic and stylistic functions in discourse. Fraser (1988:22) notes, for example, that a speaker can use "well" to signal "some degree of reluctance...to recount the story." Speakers may also use "well" to preface disagreements, such as of the "yes, but" type (Pomerantz 1975), to indicate hesitancy (Schiffrin 1987), and to elicit information that the speaker has not provided in an exchange, such as when being asked a direct question (Fraser 1988; Schiffrin 1987).

In the bilingual courtroom, pragmatic markers such as "well" are often used by witnesses to signal disagreement with part or all of the content of an attorney's question or statement:

(2) A: A true statement, a correct statement, would be to say that, uh, the FED
     establishes a minimum price for milk to the farmers.
     W: Bueno, desde, alrededor del 2000 entiendo que ellos decidieron es-
     tablecer un precio mínimo por cada galón de leche que producen.
     (Well, since around 2000 I believe that they decided to establish a mini-
     mum price per gallon for the milk they produce.)
     I: Since around 2000 I believe that they established a minimum price per
     gallon for the milk produced.

In this example, the attorney who is cross-examining the plaintiff is attempting to obtain a definite answer from him. The attorney's statement implies that the witness knows about the FED's role in price setting, but is not being forward with his responses. The witness initiates his response with the marker *bueno* (well) to signal that although the attorney's assumptions about the FED's role are correct, they are only partly so. The FED started to regulate the price of milk in 2000, which is after the plaintiffs brought suit against the defendant. In this case, the defendant was a government-subsidized producer of milk.

Attorneys, on the other hand, may use the discourse marker "well" to signal to the witness or plaintiff that he or she has not provided the desired response. In the courtroom, witnesses are expected to "respond to the questions asked. If witnesses do not follow the question frame or elaborate the answer further than requested, their answers are considered dispreferred or unexpected turns" (Rigney 1997:124). A dispreferred answer may prompt the attorney to preface a subsequent question with a discourse marker such as "well":

(3) A: The other three people that you mentioned yesterday, but you didn't recall their names, did they drink?

I: Y las tres—y las tres personas que usted mencionó ayer, pero sus nombres no recordó, ¿esas personas ingirieron alcohol?

W: ¿Las muchachas?

I: The girls, are you asking?

A: *Well*, you mentioned one name who was a driver. Who was that? What was his name? Could you tell the members of the jury the name of this person?

(Bueno, usted mencionó un nombre que era un conductor. ¿Quién era ese? ¿Cómo se llamaba? Le podría decir a los miembros del jurado el nombre de esta persona?)

I: Usted mencionó el nombre del conductor. ¿Quién era ese? ¿Cómo se llamaba? Podría decirle a los miembros del jurado el nombre de esta persona?)

Here the attorney seems surprised with the witness's request for clarification, as in *las muchachas?* (the girls?), because he expects the witness to know to whom he is referring. To express his surprise and disbelief he prefaces his answer with the marker "well" in order to assert his need for an appropriate response and, more importantly, to reestablish control over the exchange and over the topics discussed. The attorney's disbelief, however, is lost in the interpreter's rendition. The interpreter is unable to recall the attorney's use of a turn-initial discourse marker. The interpreter's omission is triggered by a lack of recall and possibly by its utterance-initial status. Because this omission changes the tone of the original, the attorney cannot convey, as forcefully as he intends, his lack of confidence in the witness's statements.

Politeness Markers

Brown and Levinson (1987) developed a theory of politeness that builds on Goffman's (1967) ideas about face work. This theory explains how each individual has a need to promote both a positive and a negative face. Speakers promote their positive face through the use of *positive politeness*. Positive politeness allows speakers to project a self that is empathetic and affiliated with others. Speakers promote their negative face using speech acts that recognize the speakers' imposition on the addressees, as conveyed in the term "please," and the need for formality and deference, as conveyed in terms of address such as "sir" and "ma'am" and titles of address such as "Mr." or "Mrs." In a legal setting, such as during the course of a trial, counsel can use *negative politeness* to build a rapport with a witness:

(4) A: *Sir*, did you go to the party?
     I: *Señor*, usted fue a la fiesta?
     W: Sí, señor.
     I: Yes, sir.

In the data, the interpreter's faithful rendition of a mode of address, such as "sir," is observed most often when two conditions are met, the mode of address or politeness marker is in utterance-final position and, the marker appears in short turns of talk (seven or fewer words). In longer turns of talk (ten or more words), formal modes of address, such as "sir," that appear in onset-initial position are omitted in almost every instance:

(5) A: *Sir*, although this paragraph states that you and your wife visit your
        children in Florida and on vacation, the truth of the matter is that your
        wife lives with your children in Florida. Is that correct?
        (Señor, a pesar de que este párrafo indica que usted y su esposa visitaban
        a sus hijos en la Florida y durante las vacaciones, el hecho es que su es-
        posa vive con sus hijos en la Florida, ¿no es eso cierto?)
        I: A pesar de que ahí dice que su esposa viaja con usted a visitar a los
        niños y durante las vacaciones a la Florida, la verdad es que su esposa
        vive con sus hijos en la Florida, ¿no es cierto?

The cost of the interpreter's omission is observed in its effect on counsel's strategy. In example 5, the defense attorney, who is in the process of cross-examining the plaintiff, uses the politeness marker "sir" during a very confrontational and face-threatening part of the cross-examination. He uses "sir" as part of his legal strategy to accomplish two tasks: confront the witness, which is face-threatening, and avoid being judged as harsh and disrespectful by the jury, which is face-saving. The interpreter's rendition, which does not include the form of address "sir," omits a key part of the defense's cross-examination strategy and challenges the forceful, yet respectful, tone of the original.

Although less frequently observed in the data, the length of a turn may also prompt the interpreter to add a politeness marker, *por favor* (please) to the original. The addition of a politeness marker may reduce the rate of imposition of the attorney's question on the witness:

(6) A: You say that you heard a noise and ran out of the house to see what was going on. Would you explain to me when and where that happened? (Usted dice que escuchó un ruido y salió de la casa corriendo para ver que estaba sucediendo ¿Usted me puede explicar cuándo y dónde sucedió eso?)
I: Usted dice que oyó un ruido y salió de la casa corriendo para ver que estaba sucediendo ¿Usted nos puede explicar, *por favor*, cuándo y dónde sucedió eso?

The opposing attorney, although not overtly hostile towards the witness, did not chose to use a politeness marker, such as *por favor* (please), in his line of questioning. The interpreter's addition of this politeness marker, thus, creates a false sense of civility and respect that is not intended in the attorney's original question. In this example, the interpreter's rendition changes the type of rapport the attorney wishes to establish with the witness. That is, from a direct rapport to a face saving one that is aimed at softening the tone of the attorney's line of questioning.

It is important to note that the interpreters' additions and omissions of politeness markers were observed most often during the attorneys' cross-examination of witnesses. This is not surprising because the data reflects that attorneys seem to ask the lengthiest and most linguistically dense questions when cross-examining witnesses. In this study, counsel's cross-examination of witnesses seems to have been used to either overwhelm the witness or intimidate him or her. The effect of counsel's strategy is that it also seems to have overwhelmed the interpreter's processing ability. A more detailed description of the interpreter's approach to counsel's strategy will be provided in Chapter 4.

Topic Management

The discourse marker "now" serves to signal a discourse transition and "a refocusing on a part of the topic at hand" (Fraser 1988:23). This discourse marker plays an essential role during an attorney's examination of a witness, because it directs the witness's attention from a previous topic to a new one. This topic marker, although essential for legal strategy, is consistently omitted at higher turn lengths:

(7) A: Did—did you see José during those days?
    I: ¿Usted vio, eh, a José durante esos días?
    W: Sí.
    I: Yes.
    A: *Now*, you mentioned that you were also hit, uh, uh, during that incident; that the police officer hit you many times. Uh, during the night and the following days, how did you feel—how did you feel physically as the result of those injuries?
    (Ahora, usted mencionó que usted también había sido golpeado, eh, eh, durante ese incidente, que el policía le dio muchas veces. Ah, durante la noche y los días subsiguientes, ¿cómo se sintió usted—cómo se sintió físicamente como resultado de esos golpes?)
    I: Usted dijo que usted fue agredido también. Que el policía le dio varias veces. ¿Cómo se sintió—se sintió usted físicamente en esos días subsiguientes?

The attorney for the plaintiff uses the topic marker "now" so as to accomplish two goals: first, to mark the refocusing of the topic at hand and, second, to maintain control of the exchange. In this example, the attorney wishes to guide the witness to what Hale (2004:66) denotes as "the right direction." On this occasion, the interpreter's omission results in the attorney being less effective in maintaining a cohesive line of questioning that clearly ties the plaintiff's claims of police brutality, that is, those he made earlier in his testimony, with the witness's own experiences with the municipal police on the day of the plaintiff's alleged assault. The cost associated with a longer utterance is the failure to maintain those linguistic features that, though not contributing to the syntactic meaning of the original, contribute greatly to the attorney's strategic management of the witness.

SYNTAX

Languages follow a great deal of variation with respect to how the elements of a sentence are ordered. In both Spanish and English, speakers can order the elements of a sentence to "mark as topic the referent that the message is about" (Levelt 1983:151). The speaker may convey this information using the active construction or, alternatively, the passive construction. The latter entails the promotion of one element of a sentence, such as an object, to subject position:

(8) John broke the glass. (active)
    The glass was broken by John. (passive)

In the active construction, the semantic and syntactic subject "John" is topicalized and, thus, is more salient. In this type of construction the listeners' attention is focused on "John" rather than on the object "glass." In the passive construction, on the other hand, the semantic object "glass" has been promoted to subject position and is, thus, more syntactically salient than the agent "John." This process of promotion and demotion demonstrates how speakers give priority treatment to one element of a sentence, as, for example, the subject of a sentence, through grammatical encoding (Levelt 1983:152).

In addition to the "true" passive construction (*be* + *past participle* construction), the passive construction in Spanish can be expressed also using a variety of passive-like constructions. In Spanish, there are two syntactic constructions that can be used in lieu of the "true" passive: the reflexive passive and the dative of interest. The reflexive passive is a syntactic construction that uses the reflexive particle "se" in place of the passive voice (Berk-Seligson 2002:101-102; Ramsey 1956:385). It is used with inanimate subjects that cannot act upon themselves and are acted upon by an agent (Solé and Solé 1977:81). The dative of interest and the "se me" construction (Berk-Seligson 2002:102; Lado and Blansitt 1967:63; Mujica 1982:35; Solé and Solé 1977:82; Soto 1969:255) are used to refer to events that are unplanned, unintended, and unexpected.

Examples of the "reflexive passive" and the "dative of interest," respectively, include the following:

(9)   Se rompió la mesa. (The table broke.)
(10) Se me rompió la mesa (a mí.) (The table broke [on me].)

In examples 9 and 10, the semantic object, *la mesa* (the table), does not designate an agent who does something, but rather designates an experiencer (Seco 1996:182). It is as if *the table* broke on its own volition, rather than it broke because someone acted upon it.

Speakers can also change the basic word order of a sentence through either object-fronting or the fronting of an interrogative phrase. The promotion of a linguistic constituent, though a syntactic operation, also provides more discourse saliency to that specific constituent. The opposite would hold true with the demotion of a linguistic constituent. In the bilingual courtroom, cognitive overload seems to account for a portion of the interpreters' deviations from the syntactic properties of the original.

Active and Passive Constructions

Although Spanish speakers often use passive constructions, particularly the "reflexive" passive, in this study neither the witnesses nor the interpreters used these types of constructions often. Witnesses preferred to use the active construction in their testimony and, in those instances in which they used the passive, they opted for the "true" passive construction. The interpreters in this study most often followed the witnesses' lead, to the extent that English syntactical rules allowed, and opted to use also the active construction or the "true" passive construction in their renditions. The interpreters, however, on occasion chose their grammatical constructions independently of whether the witnesses had used the active or passive forms. This was evidenced most often with turns that were thirteen words or higher:

(11) W: *El policía no le dijo nada a mi hermano*. Ni que lo iban a llevar al tribunal al otro día ni que nosotros debíamos estar presente allí. No le dijo absolutamente nada a él. No se porque lo trataron así.
     (The police officer did not say anything to my brother. Neither that he would be taken to court the next day nor that we should be present there. He didn't say anything to him. I don't know why they treated him like that.)
     I: *My brother was not told anything*. Neither that he would be taken to court the next day nor that we should be present there. Nothing was said to him. I don't know why he was treated like that.

The interpreter's use of the passive construction took the focus and responsibility away from the police officer who, according to the witness, did not fulfill his responsibilities. In the original utterance, the witness is clear in placing direct blame on the police officer for his brother not knowing that he would be taken to court the next day. In the interpreter's rendition, the police officer is not directly to blame. The interpreter's treatment of grammatical case, thus, appears to act as what Berk-Seligson (2002:114) calls a blame avoidance mechanism.

In this study, the close examination of the properties of the entire utterance seems to suggest that changes in grammatical case may have been triggered by two factors: the turn-initial status of the passive construction and the length of the utterance. All of the examples included in the data that show interpreters changing the grammatical construction of the original were observed at either utterance-initial or utterance-medial position and with lengthier utterances, specifically utterances that were thirteen words or longer. Shorter utterances did not seem to exhibit a significant change in grammatical case.

Promotion and Demotion

Although changes in grammatical case are classic examples of fronting, interpreters in the data also promoted other linguistic constituents such as interrogatives that are positioned at the end of the attorneys' utterances:

(12) A: And what did you see when you say they were hitting him? You say that he was on the ground while the police were hitting him. *Could you please describe more in detail what you saw?*
(¿Y qué fue lo que usted vio cuando usted dice que le estaban pegando a él? Usted dice que él estaba en el suelo cuando la policía le estaba golpeando. ¿Podría describir en más detalle lo que usted vio?)
I: *¿Podría describir con más detalle que fue lo que usted vio* cuando usted dice que vio a la policía agrediendo a su hermano? Usted dice que su hermano estaba en el suelo cuando la policía le estaba dando.

In example 12, the attorney for the plaintiff is asking the plaintiff's brother a series of questions that are meant to elucidate what had transpired the night the police allegedly assaulted the plaintiff. In this turn of talk, the interpreter promotes the second of the two interrogatives, which may have been fresher in the interpreter's memory than the first. The cost to the original is that the interpreter's changes give the second interrogative more discourse saliency.

The increased demands on memory seem to have prompted the court interpreters in this study to order, and specifically promote, some of the information they received in a manner that is unlike the original utterance. In this study, better recall of final constituents in a phrase, particularly as utterance-length rises, seems to have been the motivating force in interpreters' use of promotion and fronting. This behavior appears to be consistent with Isham and Lane's (1994:248) findings, which propose that more information remains available for the final clause or constituent in a segment of speech than for previous ones.

MEANING

Courtroom interpreters often place a great deal of attention to capturing the meaning of lexical items. Although a focus on form is often not encouraged because it may lead to inaccurate translations (Gile 1995; Seleskovitch 1978; González, Vázques, and Mikkelson 1991), court interpreters face a difficult task when trying to keep their renditions as close as possible to the original. In this study, high turn length seems to contribute significantly to the interpreters' inability to recall lexical items in a turn of talk, as is illustrated in the following example:

(13) A: Would you explain to the court what is the purpose of the FED? What you just made reference to in your testimony.

W: La FED es una agencia que regula el precio para la leche que producen los ganaderos. La FED establece un precio *fijo* que son 10 centavos por galón de leche fresca. Este es el precio que paga *X*. Nosotros pagamos 52 centavos.

(The FED is an agency that regulates the price of milk that dairy farmers produce. The FED establishes a fixed price, which is 10 cents per gallon of fresh milk. This is the price that *X* pays. We pay 52 cents.)

I: The FED is an agency that regulates the price of milk that farmers produce. The FED establishes a price, which is 10 cents per gallon of fresh milk. This is what *X* pays. We pay 52 cents.

This type of testimony is observed during counsel's direct examination of an expert witness. As this example shows, expert testimony can be lengthy and textually dense. Although high textual density or complexity does not need to be correlated with the length of an utterance (Palma 1995), in this study the two are very often related and may have contributed to the interpreter omitting lexical modifiers, such as fixed (price).

The interpreters' use of lexical items whose meaning did not match well the original is observed also as utterance length increases. The linguistic effect of the interpreters' lexical changes carries a cost, which compromises the specificity of an utterance and, on occasion, its legal relevance:

(14) W: Mi hermano estaba en el suelo y esos oficiales estaban dándole. Yo le pedí que dejaran de darle a mi hermano, pero ellos seguían dandole puños, patadas, *agrediéndole*. No dejaban de darle.

(My brother was on the ground, and those officers were hitting him. I asked them to stop hitting my brother, but they kept punching him, kicking him, assaulting him. They wouldn't stop hitting him.)

I: My brother was on the pavement, and those officers were hitting him. I asked them to stop hitting my brother. They kept punching him, kicking him, *attacking* him. They wouldn't stop hitting him.

In example 14, the attorney for the plaintiff begins his direct examination by asking the plaintiff's brother to describe for the jury what transpired the night of the plaintiff's alleged assault. The witness testifies that his brother was on the floor when the police officers were hitting and assaulting him. The witness uses the term *agredir*[1] (assault) to describe his impression of the police's arrest of the plaintiff. The witness could have used the verb *atacar* or (attack) to describe the actions of the police; however, throughout his testimony he used the verb *agredir* or (assault). The latter can be used as a legal term, in both Spanish and English, to indicate a person's offensive or violent touching of another. In this case, the police's offensive handling of the plaintiff. This meaning is lost, however, in the interpreter's rendition, because the verb "attack" does not carry the same legal weight as "assault." In this sense, the density of the plaintiff's utterance, coupled with its length, may have contributed to the interpreter not focusing on the legal meaning of the term *agredir* (assault). The interpreter seems to have placed more significance on the general theme of the plaintiff's testimony, that is, the police's alleged beating, rather than on the potential legal ramifications of the police's alleged behavior or assault.

INTENT

Interpreters through their additions can change the pragmatic intent of the original utterance. These changes can have at its source the violation of Grice's (1975) maxims. Grice developed the concept of *implicature*, which describes how people use language effectively. He notes that there is a set of assumptions that guide how people communicate with each other. These assumptions allow for the effective use of language, which further a cooperative end between a speaker and his or her addressee. He named these guidelines the *maxims of cooperation*. One of these maxims is the *maxim of quantity*. The *maxim of quantity* states that the speaker should make his or her contribution as is required by the context and purpose of the conversational exchange. A violation of this maxim would include the speaker providing more or, alternatively, less information than is required for the conversational exchange.

In the bilingual courtroom, this maxim is often violated when the interpreter does not use the witnesses' or attorneys' utterances as the measure from which to determine what is required for a particular rendition. The data for this study shows that interpreters violated the cooperative maxim to either "insert linguistic material that is perceived to be underlying or 'understood' in the original utterances" (Berk-Seligson 2002:131) or to "add substance that cannot be seen by an observer to be underlying the witness's abbreviated answer" (Berk-Seligson 2002:134). In both of these scenarios, the interpreter violates the maxim of quantity through their addition of entire phrases or sentences rather than just linguistic markers. This is observed, on average, in turns of talk that exceed ten words:

(15) A: Did you get to meet with the, uh, upcoming director at that time?
W: Sí.
I: Yes.
A: Could you describe to us who, if anyone, is that person? Did you ever talk to her about the problems at the hotel or about your problems with Mr. X? How do you know her?
(Podría usted describirnos, ¿quién, si acaso alguien, es esa persona? Alguna vez le habló de los problemas en el hotel o de sus problemas con el señor X. ¿Cómo la conoce a ella?)
I: ¿Quién, si acaso alguien, es la persona esa? *La directora.* Alguna vez le habló de los problemas en el hotel o de los problemas con el señor X. ¿Cómo la conoce a ella?

In this example, the attorney introduces the topic "the upcoming director" in his first turn of talk. His second question, which builds from the previous one, includes the referent "that person." The latter establishes a semantic relationship with the previously mentioned topic, "the upcoming director," and, thus, serves as its co-referent. The interpreter's rendition of the attorney's question is fairly accurate, until the interpreter adds the referent *la directora* (the director). The interpreter's addition of this referent, although grammatically unnecessary, suggests that the interpreter, possibly as a result of processing a lot of information, wants to close the "referential distance" (Givón 1983:354) between the referent, "the upcoming director," and its co-referent, "that person." The motivation behind the interpreter's actions is possibly to be more precise, in light of increased cognitive overload.

The interpreter also adds information to her rendition that is not stated or implied in the plaintiff's answer:

(16) A: From that table, Mrs. B, my question is, do you see any clerical positions in the proposal?
I: Mi pregunta Sra. B es, si—¿qué si de esa tabla se desprende que hubiesen puestos clericales en la propuesta?
W: A mí se me dijo que podía regresar a trabajar. Yo no sé si esa tabla incluye puestos de oficina, pero si sé que cuando a mí me despidieron me dijeron que habría trabajo despúes del primero de enero. *Lo de la tabla, sinceramente no sé.*
(I was told that I could come back to work. I don't know if that table includes office positions, but I do know that when I was let go I was told

that there would be work after the first of January. About the table, I sincerely don't know.)

I: I was told that I could come back to work. I don't know if the table includes clerical positions, but I do know that when I was laid off, I was told that there would be work after the first of January. *I don't know about the table. I sincerely would be amenable to tell you.*

In example 16, the witness states that she cannot tell from the exhibit whether there were any clerical positions available in the proposal. The interpreter took the liberty to add information to the plaintiff's answer that is neither conveyed nor implied in the original. Although these types of additions are not observed often in the data, they create the impression that the witness is challenging the attorney. The interpreter's rendition went beyond what was required for the plaintiff's response of *sinceramente no sé* (I sincerely don't know) and became a confrontational response in the line of "I don't know, but if I did, which you (the attorney) seem to think I do, I would be happy to tell you." This type of addition violates the cooperative principle (Grice 1975: 45), because the interpreter introduces information in her rendition that is more than is required for the exchange and that results in an implied and confrontational meaning not intended by the plaintiff. As with all other examples that include a violation of Grice's maxim of quantity, these occur at increasing turn lengths.

An explanation of the interpreter's linguistic behavior, in the sections that deal with the interpreters' rendition of style, meaning, and intent, suggest that, in addition to considering the relationship between interpreters' renditions and the legal process, researchers and practitioners need to consider the extent to which interpreters' performance is adversely affected by cognitive overload.

The following section will examine the extent of the relationship between the length of an utterance and the quality of interpreters' renditions, which cannot be determined solely through a qualitative analysis. The results of this analysis, particularly if I find a significant relationship, could be used to direct the efforts of court interpreters, and those who train them, to more cognitive-based approaches that minimize interpreters' intrusiveness in the courtroom.

EXAMINING COGNITIVE OVERLOAD: THE TRUE RELATIONSHIP BETWEEN LINGUISTIC VARIABLES AND TURN LENGTH

To start the analysis, I quantify the number of interpreter-induced errors observed in the data. This analysis examines all additions, omissions, and

Table 3.1.   Distribution of Dependent Variables

Type of error	Additions	Omissions	Changes
Dependent Variables			
Politeness Markers	6	67	
Forms of Address	58	120	
Active to Passive			42
Passive to Active			30
Focus Change			36
Verb Change			80
Lexical Change			112
Speech Disfluencies	2,925	2,839	
Hedges "Well"	32	148	
Discourse Markers	38	869	
General Statements	27		
Total	3,086	4,043	300

changes in 3,317 turns of talk. The results that are presented in Table 3.1 indicate that the majority of interpreter-induced errors are those in which the interpreter adds or omits linguistic markers that assign tone and style to the original, such as speech disfluencies and discourse markers. The results also suggest that interpreters omit more linguistic content than they add, while providing their renditions.

Once the data is quantified and classified, I perform a regression analysis[2] that examines the relationship between the interpreter's additions, omissions, and changes and turn length. The benefit of using a regression analysis rather than a correlation analysis is that it allowed me to test whether a set of variables (dependent) is significantly correlated to turn length (independent) and the amount (estimated coefficient) and rate (adjusted R-squared) of the errors explained by turn length.

The results[3] of the regression analysis show that the relationship is significant ($t \geq 2.0$) for each individual linguistic variable. Although the relationship is significant, each individual variable accounts for a small percentage of the errors ($< 5\%$). The error rate, however, rose when the data was combined to account for total events or total errors. In this regression, the relationship between turn length and the linguistic variables is significant and not random. Table 3.2 summarizes these results.

The results show that at least one event (either an addition, omission, or change) should be expected whenever the length of an utterance is seven words or greater. I arrive at this result by multiplying the estimated coefficient on turn length (0.26) by seven words and by adding the estimated coefficient on the constant (-0.61).[4] The choice to use seven words was based, in part, on the findings of prior research on the capacity of short-term memory, STM,

Table 3.2. Dependent Variable: Total Events

	Parameters	Constant	Turn Length
Estimated Parameters			
Estimated Coefficient		–0.61643	0.26044
T-Statistic		(4.56721)	(17.5533)
Adjusted R-squared	0.37523		

(Atkinson & Schiffrin 1968; Miller 1956; Smith 1985), which suggests that STM is very limited and may store only around seven items, or chunks of information, at a time. Other turn lengths could have been chosen as well and would have resulted also in positive additions or omissions.

The adjusted R-squared indicates that the length of a turn "explains" approximately 38 percent of the observed errors. In lay terms, this result shows that if there were 1,000 errors of the linguistic variables tested, 380 of these errors would be attributed to longer turn lengths.

In addition to examining the effect of the length of a turn on total events, I also examine the effect of turn length on total additions and total omissions. I did not include in this part of the analysis total changes, because this variable, when compared with total additions and omissions accounts for a small, albeit significant, portion of the errors. Tables 3.3 and 3.4 present the regression results for total additions and total omissions.

Both the regression of total additions and the regression of total omissions on the length of a turn have significant t-statistics. The adjusted R-squared statistics for total additions and total omissions are approximately 15 percent and 33 percent respectively. These R-squared results indicate that the length of a turn is better at explaining the interpreters' error rates of omissions than it is at explaining the interpreters' additions. These results also suggest that an interpreter's ability to recall linguistic variables in an utterance deteriorates more rapidly as turn length increases. These findings complement those of Linell, Wadenjö and Jönsson (1992:127), who discovered that cognitive factors prompted interpreters to often condense the source language discourse by omitting linguistic variables, such as hesitations and discourse markers.

Table 3.3. Dependent Variable: Total Additions

	Parameters	Constant	Turn Length
Estimated Parameters			
Estimated Coefficient		0.34562	0.09284
T-Statistic		(3.14386)	(15.61070)
Adjusted R squared	0.15046		

Table 3.4.   Dependent Variable: Total Omissions

	Parameters	Constant	Turn Length
Estimated Parameters			
Estimated Coefficient		0.28001	0.13284
T-Statistic		(11.75021)	(11.54232)
Adjusted R-squared	0.33300		

The final step at estimating the true relationship between turn length and error rates in interpreters' renditions is to segment the data for a variety of turn lengths. The turn lengths that were tested include[5] those with six or fewer words and ten or more words. This refinement of the estimates reveals whether the error rates rise at a constant rate or, as I suspect, whether they increase at an accelerating rate as the length of an utterance rises. An increasing, rather than a constant, error rate indicates that the error rate to turn length relationship is non linear. For instance, if the rate is increasing, there may be only one error for the first ten words, but two additional errors for the next two words, and four additional errors for the last ten words, which would give us a total of seven errors for a 30-word utterance. Table 3.5 includes the results of the analysis for total events, which indicate non linearity.

The results show that interpreters in the study make 0.137 errors per word for utterances that have six or fewer words. Stated another way, if I observe 100 six-word utterances, I should expect to have 82.3 additions and omissions, which is the product of the estimated coefficient by six, in those 100 six-word utterances. When the length of a turn increases to ten or more words, the interpreters' errors rise to 0.305, which is over twice the rate that is observed with six or fewer words. This pattern held at a constant and increasing rate for values over 13 words.

The error patterns observed for total additions and total omissions also show a significant rate of errors as turn length goes from six or fewer words

Table 3.5.   Summary of Regression Results for Total Events

Estimated Parameters	*Estimated Coefficient*	*t-statistic*	*Adjusted R-squared*
Parameters			
Turn Length (≤ 6 words)	0.13718	7.64470	0.04307
Turn Length (≥ words)	0.28410	11.6482	0.30766
Turn Length (≤ 9 words)	0.18893	13.7708	0.10464
Turn Length (≥ 10 words)	0.30514	9.76140	0.30185
Turn Length (≤ 12 words)	0.26998	17.2974	0.12074
Turn Length (≥ 13 words)	0.59784	7.58979	0.24298

Table 3.6.   Summary of Regression Results for Total Additions

Estimated Parameters	Estimated Coefficient	t-statistic	Adjusted R-squared
Parameters			
Turn Length (≤ 6 words)	0.07650	17.3002	0.01967
Turn Length (≥ 7 words)	0.10447	10.8039	0.10790
Turn Length (≤ 9 words)	0.08434	7.99872	0.03583
Turn Length (≥ 10 words)	0.12977	6.23334	0.12355
Turn Length (≤ 12 words)	0.07125	9.10340	0.03726
Turn Length (≥ 13 words)	0.12221	7.20110	0.27567

to ten or more words, as illustrated in Tables 3.6 and 3.7. The differences between these two variables, however, lie in the extent of the error rates. In the case of additions error rates rise at a relatively constant rate, whereas for omissions they rise at an increasing rate. These results have both linguistic and cognitive connotations.

From a linguistic perspective, it suggests that interpreters will omit more of the linguistic variables that assign style and tone to the original as turn length increases. The omission of linguistic variables that shape the register of the original, for some turns of talk, may change the register of the witness's utterances from *powerless* to *powerful*. The latter may benefit the witness in the eyes of jurors and, possibly, alter the outcome of a trial.

From a cognitive perspective, the results suggest that there may be significant cognitive differences in the manner in which interpreters respond to increased demands on memory. The cost of cognitive overload, as turn length increases, on the interpreting process seems to be more significant for loss of recall than for the need to embellish or compensate. Some possible explanations for the interpreters' increased rate of omissions may include the interpreter choosing, consciously or unconsciously, to omit those linguistic variables that he or she finds meaningless or that occur at the onset of an utterance.

Table 3.7.   Summary of Regression Results for Total Omissions

Estimated Parameters	Estimated Coefficient	t-statistic	Adjusted R-squared
Parameters			
Turn Length (≤ 6 words)	0.06087	17.3002	0.04794
Turn Length (≥ 7 words)	0.18963	7.40917	0.27137
Turn Length (≤ 9 words)	0.10490	13.0765	0.11587
Turn Length (≥ 10 words)	0.20517	2.44715	0.04139
Turn Length (≤ 12 words)	0.09872	16.6422	0.12813
Turn Length (≥ 13 words)	0.28562	4.86025	0.21467

Qualitative examination of the data, for example, appears to indicate that linguistic content is omitted more often when it occurs at the onset of an utterance than when it occurs at the end of an utterance. To test this theory, I performed a regression analysis of the linguistic variables that occur at onset-initial and turn-final position. The results for turn-final linguistic omissions are not statistically significant. The results for onset-initial linguistic variables, on the other hand, are significant and suggest that as turn length increases, speech disfluencies, discourse markers, and politeness markers are omitted at a statistically increasing, rather than a constant, rate. Table 3.8

Table 3.8. Summary of Regression Results for Speech Disfluencies, Discourse Markers, and Politeness Markers at Onset-Initial Position

Speech Disfluencies			
Estimated Parameters	*Estimated Coefficient*	*t-statistic*	*Adjusted R-squared*
Parameters			
Turn Length (≤ 6 words)	0.23410	6.76543	0.02652
Turn Length (≥ 7 words)	0.34340	17.2889	0.29001
Turn Length (≤ 9 words)	0.16732	10.7103	0.11876
Turn Length (≥ 10 words)	0.29007	11.7642	0.29010
Turn Length (≤ 12 words)	0.15432	16.2019	0.13427
Turn Length (≥ 13 words)	0.43121	8.51131	0.47634

Discourse Markers			
Estimated Parameters	*Estimated Coefficient*	*t-statistic*	*Adjusted R-squared*
Parameters			
Turn Length (≤ 6 words)	0.06350	14.3004	0.05437
Turn Length (≥ 7 words)	0.24446	11.8049	0.18866
Turn Length (≤ 9 words)	0.06734	4.99872	0.02456
Turn Length (≥ 10 words)	0.18787	6.45334	0.21987
Turn Length (≤ 12 words)	0.17325	8.10356	0.02453
Turn Length (≥ 13 words)	0.36321	9.20340	0.36574

Politeness Markers			
Estimated Parameters	*Estimated Coefficient*	*t-statistic*	*Adjusted R-squared*
Parameters			
Turn Length (≤ 6 words)	0.03456	18.3000	0.04210
Turn Length (≥ 7 words)	0.18796	6.40812	0.30176
Turn Length (≤ 9 words)	0.10336	14.0654	0.12166
Turn Length (≥ 10 words)	0.30287	3.00321	0.11665
Turn Length (≤ 12 words)	0.11765	14.7530	0.14213
Turn Length (≥ 13 words)	0.24543	3.82345	0.32001

presents these results. Although the results on Table 3.8 appear to indicate that the position of a discourse marker is a significant factor in its recall, further study is needed to establish conclusively whether the position of linguistic variables in a turn of talk affects interpreters' rate of omissions. In Chapter 6, I examine whether an interpreter's gender plays a role in his or her successful rendition of turn-initial or turn-final linguistic variables.

SUMMARY

The interpreting and legal profession expects interpreters to provide a faithful rendition of courtroom discourse. This requires that the interpreter convey every element in an utterance, which includes a fairly verbatim account of pauses, hesitations, and other pragmatic and extralinguistic content. Interpreters, however, are frequently unable to fulfill this expectation. The interpreters' failure to abide by the requirement of providing a faithful rendition often results in changes to the register and style of the original. These changes may alter jurors' perception of a witness or of counsel in a positive or detrimental way. Either scenario may affect the outcome of a trial.

The significance of the linguistic and legal connotations of interpreted testimony attested in prior research prompted me to investigate the possible cognitive reasons for some of the interpreters' treatment of key linguistic variables. The main findings of this research point to the significant relationship that seems to hold between utterance length and interpreters' treatment of style, syntax, meaning, and intent. The results of the analysis show that turn length explains about 38 percent of the total errors observed in the data. This rate increased with the segmentation of the data and shows that the error rate for total omissions increases at an increasing rather than a constant rate. These findings have both linguistic and cognitive implications, because they suggest that the effect of turn length on memory is detrimental and may result in the interpreter altering the register of the original, as, for example, from a *powerless* to a *powerful* speech style. In light of prior studies, the effects of cognitive overload on the interpreting process seem to be even more significant than may have been previously thought. There are potential legal ramifications with the interpreter's linguistic response to cognitive overload.

In sum, the findings of this study suggest that researchers and practitioners of courtroom interpreting may need to direct their efforts more aggressively to finding strategies that assist in reducing cognitive overload. Future studies that examine the relationship between turn length and the quality of interpreters' renditions should be performed also to confirm these findings and to account for other possible sources of errors, such as cultural, gender, and linguistic differences. The researcher could use the regression analysis techniques discussed in the Appendices to test the effect, and explanatory power, of multiple variables on the interpreting process.

NOTES

1. Assault is defined as the crime of physically attacking another person in such a way that results in serious bodily harm and/or is made with a deadly or dangerous weapon such as a gun, knife, sword, ax, or blunt instrument. Aggravated assault is usually a felony punishable by a term in state prison.

2. See Appendix 3.

3. See Appendix 4.

4. $-0.61 + 7 \cdot (0.26) > 1$

5. The turn lengths tested include 6 or fewer words, 7 or more words, 9 or fewer words, 10 or more words, 12 or fewer words, and 13 or more words.

Chapter Four

Counteracting The Effects of Cognitive Overload: The Interpreters' Use of Interruptions and Semiconsecutive Interpreting

Chapter 3 examined the negative effect that turn length has on the interpreters' ability to provide a faithful rendition of the original discourse. I present evidence that suggests that as the length of an utterance grows, the interpreters' ability to perform their duties up to the standards and expectations of their profession and of the legal community declines significantly. Most courtroom interpreters recognize the effects of length on their ability to perform their duties, and they develop strategies to counteract these effects. This chapter will examine two strategies that courtroom interpreters in this study use to contend with the high demands that the interpreting process places on their memory: the interpreters' interruption of a witness and the interpreters' use of the semiconsecutive mode. The purpose of this analysis is to describe the possible uses, benefits, and limitations of two strategies that interpreters often use to counteract the effects of turn length on their performance.

THE EFFECT OF INTERRUPTIONS IN THE BILINGUAL COURTROOM

A strategy commonly used by interpreters to manage cognitive overload is to interrupt the attorney or witness. Mikkelson (1989:11), for example, notes that interpreters exercise their right to interrupt witnesses and attorneys quite often in the bilingual courtroom. She based her conclusions on the results of a poll of federally certified court interpreters conducted in the late 1980s, which found that of 127 interpreters surveyed, 85 percent said they interrupt witnesses or attorneys either sometimes, often, or at every interpreting event. Only 33 percent responded that they rarely or never interrupt.

In this study, the interpreters remarked that they were not averse to using interruptions and found this strategy to be of assistance with speech that was dense or voluminous. The interpreters, however, were observed interrupting only witnesses, particularly non-expert witnesses. It seems that the hierarchical nature of the courts, and possibly cultural factors, affected the interpreter's choice to interrupt. In the next sections, I examine the uses of the interpreters' interruptions and the effectiveness of this strategy at reducing interpreter-induced errors.

How Interpreters Interrupt

When the interpreters in this study anticipated a high-length utterance, or high-textual density, the main strategy that they used to counteract the effects of these utterances on their processing capacity was to interrupt the witness. These interruptions occurred at three points in discourse: before the witness had finished uttering a sentence, after the witness had finished uttering a complete sentence or grammatical unit, and after the witness had provided an answer that included various complex sentences or clauses. The first of these types of interruptions is seen in the following example:

(1) A: So when you—when you, uh, requested, uh, when you explained this—what you are telling us here is that they approved the transfer for you?

I: ¿Entonces, eh, como nos dice usted, al usted explicárselo a ellos, pues le aprobaron el traslado?

W: Tomarían eso en consideración. *Desconozco si—*

(They could have taken that into account. I don't know if—)

I: Well, I—they must have taken it into account. *I don't know if that is it, the case.*

Here the interpreter imposes her own segmentation to the text and chooses to interrupt the witness at what could be described as an inappropriate time in the witness's testimony. The witness had not finished uttering the phrase that was to follow the clause *desconozco si* ([I] don't know if), when the interpreter decides to interrupt the witness and commence her rendition. The ill-timed interruption results in the interpreter adding, among other linguistic information, the noun phrase, *the case*, to her rendition. The interpreter's interruption of a witness at what could be described as an incomplete grammatical junction (Barik 1973) carries a cost. The interpreter adds linguistic content that she presumes is necessary to complete the utterance but that may not have been intended by the witness.

The second point in discourse that interpreters use to interrupt a witness is at the end of a complete grammatical junction:

(2) A: Could you please give us your educational background?
     I: Por favor, ¿podría darnos en breve su trasfondo edu—educativo? ¿Su educación?
     W: Sí. Tengo un grado asociado en ingeniería industrial y—
     (Yes. I have an associate's degree in industrial engineering and)
     I: I have an associate's degree in industrial engineering and—
     W: —Y un bachillerato en gerencia de materiales.
     I: And a bachelor's degree in materials management.

In example 2, the witness is asked to provide information about her educational background. The witness begins by stating that she has an associate's degree in industrial engineering. This fact is expressed in a simple sentence: *(yo) tengo un grado asociado en ingeniería industrial* (I have an associate's degree in industrial engineering), that is prefaced by an adverbial phrase *sí* (yes) and is followed by a coordinated conjunction *y* (and). The witness's use of this coordinated conjunction signals that she intends to proceed with her testimony and that she is going to add information about her educational background, specifically *that she holds a bachelor's degree in materials management*. The interpreter interrupts the witness at the point at which she utters the conjunction, possibly in anticipation of a lengthy or complex utterance. The interpreter's strategy to interrupt the witness at the end of a complete grammatical juncture, and before a conjunction, results in a fairly accurate rendition, with the exception of one omission—the adverbial phrase *sí* (yes).

The description of the two types of interruptions discussed in examples 1 and 2 is consonant with what has been observed in studies on simultaneous interpreting that examine the relationship between the unit of interpreting and an interpreter's performance. Christoffels and De Groot (2005), for example, in their discussion on the effect of input chunking in the interpreting process cite the work of Goldman-Eisler (1972) who found that

> for about 92% of these chunks the ear-voice span consisted of at least a complete noun phrase + verb phrase, from which she concluded that the verb phrase is an especially crucial part of the input chunk. Apparently, grammatical information is needed before interpreting is possible and the clause may be the favored unit in interpreting (1972:11).

These findings, when applied to the previous examples, seem to suggest that there may be favorable and less favorable times for an interpreter to interrupt a witness. In this study, when the interpreter waits for the witness to conclude "a crucial part of the input chunk" such as the verb phrase, the interpreter's performance is better. Thus, when the interpreter interrupts after the witness has uttered a complete sentence or grammatical unit, as it is observed in example 2, the results seem to indicate that the interpreter's performance, as measured by a lack of additions, omissions, or changes, is closer to the original. Ill-timed interruptions that occur before a sentence or embedded clause is uttered, as it is observed in example 1, however, prompt the interpreter to add grammatical information which, though it may be plausible given the context, reflect the interpreter's assumptions and not necessarily the intent of the witness. Unless the witness is allowed to finish his or her response, it is impossible to tell, for certain, what the witness intended to express in the source language.

The third point in discourse in which interruptions occur is when the interpreter interrupts at an appropriate grammatical juncture but waits too long to start his or her rendition. This is the most frequent point in discourse for the interpreters in this study to interrupt a witness:

(3) A: Was credit always given?
     I: ¿Y siempre le daban crédito?
     W: En el último caso que se generó de la última transferencia de B ella me indicó que no procedía el crédito y que se iban a comunicar conmigo para ver de que manera iban a proceder—
     (In the last case that was generated from B's last transfer, she indicated that the credit would not proceed and that they would contact me to see how they would proceed—)
     I: In the last case that was generated on the last, eh, eh, transaction, eh, transfer, transference of B, uh, she called me to let me know that the, uh, credit, would—wasn't in order. That wasn't going to, eh, be granted—
     W: —Pero nunca recibí la llamada de ellos.
     I: But I never received their call.

This example, which is representative of this type of interruption in the data, shows that when the length of an utterance increases, the number of complex sentences, which consist of more than one clause, also increases. These types of sentences can occur with independent clauses that are joined together by coordinating conjunctions, as, for example, *and*, or with sentences that have complement clauses, such as *that the credit would not proceed*.

The witness's use of a complex sentence lengthens the testimony considerably, which poses a problem for the interpreter. The witness's use of recursion[1] also prompts the interpreter to self-repair, to preface her reformulations with editing expressions, such as *eh* (uh), and to omit the content of the final embedded clause, *para ver de que manera iban a proceder* (to see how they would proceed). The interpreter's addition and omission of syntactic information from her renditions points to a relationship between turn length, which increases with recursion, and the interpreters' performance. These findings, albeit in the context of consecutive rather than simultaneous interpreting, also lend some support to Barik's (1973) observations on input chunking. Barik argues that if an interpreter waits too long to begin his or her rendition of the target language, it leads to omissions of all kinds and, thus, to a poorer performance.

The points in discourse at which interpreters chose to interrupt a witness are key to the success or failure of the strategy. In those few instances in which the interpreter interrupts at an appropriate grammatical juncture, the interpreter seems to deviate the least from the original. These instances, however, are not observed often, possibly because it is difficult for the interpreter to choose an appropriate juncture at which to interrupt while in the midst of performing his or her duties in the courtroom. That is, if the interpreter had to be aware that he or she needed to interrupt a witness only at certain auspicious times, this may in turn tax his or her processing capacity further and lead to errors.

In most cases, however, the interpreter either chooses to interrupt at an inappropriate grammatical juncture or waits too long to interrupt. The former may lead to errors because the interpreter chooses to interrupt when he or she expects more information from the speaker than he or she can handle. The latter may result in errors because the interpreter's processing capacity is already highly taxed when he or she decides to interrupt. The result of interrupting at high utterance lengths, which seems to be the norm, carries, for the most part, a cost and few benefits.

THE COST OF INTERRUPTING THE WITNESS: A LOOK AT THE NUMBERS

The benefit or cost of using interruptions to manage cognitive overload can be measured statistically. A strategy that is significantly correlated with reducing turn length should reduce total additions, omissions, and events (Chapter 3). The opposite would hold true with a strategy that did not reduce turn length. To estimate the cost or benefit of interpreters using interruptions, I used a regression analysis that estimates the relationship between interruptions and turn length. The findings show that interpreters, on average, wait too long to interrupt.

The estimated coefficient on interruptions plus the estimated coefficient on the constant reveals the average length of the turn of talk at which interpreters feel the need to interrupt the witness. Table 4.1 shows that interpreters wait, on average, until turn length reaches 21.75 words to make an interruption. Twenty-two words is a substantial amount of information to process when interpreters are expected to observe all the syntactic, semantic, and pragmatic

Table 4.1. Turn Length on Interruptions

Parameters	Constant	Turn Length	Interruptions
Estimated Parameters			
Estimated Coeficient	10.24673	0.01608	11.51581
T-Statistic	(7.13456)	(2.45622)	(7.07675)
Adjusted R-squared	0.02234		

content of the original. At this turn length, I expected to see an increase in both additions and omissions.

To estimate the error rate of additions and omissions per interruption and also account for non linearity, I examine the data at turn lengths of 13 or more words. Table 4.2 presents the results for additions.

Table 4.2 shows that the rate of errors is not significantly different from zero (*t* statistic is lower than 2.0) and, hence, is not statistically significant. Additions, thus, are observed randomly and do not add errors or reduce them in any significant way. The results are different for total omissions, because interruptions carry a significant cost with this variable. Table 4.3 presents these results.

The results suggest that interpreters make 0.86 omissions per every interrupted turn of talk. In lay terms, this means that for every 100 interruptions, interpreters will make 86 omissions. These omissions are the cost of the interpreters using interruptions as a means to reduce the effects of turn length on their processing ability.

The rate of errors with total omissions is consistent with the findings on the effect of turn length and was expected. Interpreters interrupt, on average, at around 22 words. When I examine the relationship between turn length and rate of errors with the entire data, interpreters omit at an increasing rate at 13 or more words. The finding that interpreters omit information when interrupting a witness indicates further that lack of recall is one the most affected cognitive factors in courtroom interpreting.

Table 4.2. Turn Lengths of Thirteen or More Words: Total Additions

Parameters	Constant	Turn Length	Interruptions
Estimated Parameters			
Estimated Coeficient	0.02497	0.021172	–0.13230
T-Statistic	(3.06126)	(20.63713)	(–1.01326)
Adjusted R-squared	–0.03228		

Table 4.3.   Turn Lengths of Thirteen or More Words: Total Omissions

Parameters	Constant	Turn Length	Interruptions
Estimated Parameters			
Estimated Coeficient	–0.71752	0.17133	0.867300
T-Statistic	(4.00126)	(11.35021)	(–2.16326)
Adjusted R-squared	-0.12238		

Although it is not surprising that lack of recall is significantly affected in consecutive interpreting, I did not expect the rate of errors to rise at an increasing rate. The repercussions of these findings may be felt most at a pragmatic level. From a pragmatics perspective, the increasing rate of omissions may translate to some of the witnesses' original utterances being altered toward a *powerful* style at a much higher rate than toward a *powerless* style. In the specific case of extralinguistic content and pragmatic markers, such as speech disfluencies and the marker "well," this may result in a more favorable outcome for the witness.

OTHER POSSIBLE COSTS ASSOCIATED WITH INTERRUPTIONS: AN EXAMINATION OF JURORS' EVALUATION OF INTERPRETERS WHO INTERRUPT

The statistical findings suggest that court interpreters should think twice before using interruptions to manage cognitive overload. This technique is often not helpful and only on those occasions in which the interpreter is able to interrupt at an appropriate grammatical juncture, which were few and far between, did it not result in a significant number of omissions. Other studies, such as Berk-Seligson's (2002), also lend support to the notion that interpreter-induced interruptions might add to the intrusiveness of the interpreter in the courtroom and lower ratings by jurors.

Berk-Seligson (2002), following the findings of O'Barr (1981, 1982) and his colleagues (O'Barr and Conley, 1976; O'Barr and Lind, 1981; Conley, O'Barr, and Lind, 1978; Lind and O'Barr, 1979) on mock jurors' evaluation of testimony style, performed an experimental study to test the effect that interpreters interrupting an attorney or a witness would have on jurors. She finds, for example, that when interpreters interrupt a witness, Hispanic mock jurors seem to form an unfavorable opinion of the witness:

Those who had heard the witness being interrupted by the interpreter (N = 99) found him to be significantly less convincing and less competent than did those who had heard the uninterrupted version of the testimony (N = 100) (Berk-Seligson, 2002:190).

Although she does not find that non-Hispanic mock jurors evaluate negatively those witnesses who are interrupted, the fact that Hispanic mock jurors form a negative opinion of the witness points to possible cultural differences in juror evaluations. These findings are important given current population trends in the United States, which may increase the presence of Hispanic jurors at trial.

Since the effect of interruptions seems to carry a significant cost when the interpreters interrupt a witness, it is also worth mentioning that Hispanic mock jurors also evaluated negatively attorneys who were interrupted in Berk-Seligson's study:

> Those who heard the version that included the interruptions (N = 105) also found the attorney to be significantly less confident . . . than did those who heard the version lacking in interruptions (N = 102). In addition, when the attorney was interrupted by the interpreter, Hispanic listeners found him significantly less intelligent (2002:188).

Although I did not observe interpreters interrupting an attorney in my data, what seems clear is that there are linguistic and possibly legal costs associated with interpreters interrupting an attorney or witness. This cost seems higher with Hispanic mock jurors than non-Hispanic groups. This finding is insightful, because many interpreters work in large metropolitan areas in the United States that have Hispanic jurors. In some jurisdictions, such as Los Angeles, New York, and South Florida, Hispanics who serve as jurors are a common occurrence. Hence, the legal interpreting profession needs to consider cognitive, legal, and cultural factors when deciding whether to interrupt a witness or an attorney. They also need to consider whether the possible benefit of limiting their memory effort through the use of interruptions outweighs the costs associated with interrupting in the courtroom.

SEMICONSECUTIVE INTERPRETING AND ITS LINGUISTIC REPRESENTATION IN THE DATA

The preferred mode of interpreting in this study is, as expected, the consecutive mode. Under the right conditions, however, interpreters can perform their renditions using the semiconsecutive (DeGroot 1997) or discontinuous (Gerver 1976) mode. In semiconsecutive interpreting, the speaker segments his or her speech, and the interpreter performs his or her renditions after each

segmented utterance. Unlike consecutive interpreting, the interpreter does not
need to wait until the speaker completely finishes his or her turn of speech to
start his or her rendition:

(4) A: Uh, what happened when, uh, Mr. V came back from vacation?
(Eh, ¿qué occurió cuando, eh, el Sr. V regresó de sus vacaciones?)
I: ¿Y qué ocurre cuando llega el señor *V* de vacaciones?
—
W: Estando presente el Señor J. L—
(While Mr. J. L. was present)
I: While Mr. J. L. was present—
W: —Eh, eh, él tuvo una discusión conmigo—
(Uh, Uh, he had a discussion with me)
I: He had an argument with me—
W: —Indicándole que él tenía—diciéndole al señor L que él tenía sus
reservas—
(Telling him that he had—telling Mr. L that he had his reservations)
I: Telling Mr. L that he had his reservations—
W: —Eh, en cuanto a mí ser jefe de personal—
(Uh, as to me being chief of personnel)
I: As to me being chief of personnel—
W: —Y que yo entonces, pues, le dije que porqué—
(And that I then, well, asked him why)
I: And then I asked him why—
W: —Y le dije también lo del salario—
(And I also told him about the salary)
I: And I also told him about the salary—
W: —Que me iban a pagar los $900—
(That they were going to pay me the $900)
I: That they were going to pay me $900—
W: —Que no era el salario que le habían pagado a M. P.
(That it was not the salary that they had paid M. P.)
I: That it was not the salary that they had paid to M. P.

In example 4, the plaintiff, who is suing her employer on the grounds of
sex and age discrimination, recounts the discussion she had with one of the
executives in her firm, Mr. V, regarding her new position as director of human
resources. The plaintiff, who, prior to her new appointment, had been the
former human resources director's secretary, tells the members of the court
about the alleged disparate treatment she received from Mr. V, who was allegedly against her new appointment. While recounting her story she segments

her output. Questions whose responses require a narrative description seem to have lent themselves well for the semiconsecutive mode of interpreting.

The qualitative analysis of the witness's narrative responses suggests that when the witness segments her speech, she does so at clear grammatical junctures. This is observed before and after a coordinated conjunction, such as *and*, or an elaborative discourse marker, such as *then*. The interpreter, in turn, uses the witness's natural grammatical or discourse markers as a cue to commence her renditions, which appears to have improved the quality of her renditions. The fact that turn length is low also seems to have contributed to the observed reduction in errors.

In the next section, I will examine whether semiconsecutive interpreting reduces the rate of additions and omissions in a significant way. The results of this analysis will provide some insights into the potential benefits or costs of this strategy. The findings will also serve as a basis from which to evaluate further the costs of interpreters using interruptions in the courtroom, as compared with using the semiconsecutive mode of interpreting.

THE POTENTIAL COSTS OR BENEFITS OF SEMICONSECUTIVE INTERPRETING

The statistical analysis of semiconsecutive interpreting follows that discussed with interruptions, but with the additional provision that the independent variable semiconsecutive interpreting will also be regressed. The initial results of the estimates are presented in Table 4.4.

The estimated coefficient on the constant is 10.2467. The results indicate that if the interpreter engages in semiconsecutive interpreting, the average turn length would decrease by 1.3 words to 8.9 words. This result is calculated as the sum of the estimated coefficient on semiconsecutive interpreting and the estimated coefficient on the constant.

When these results are compared with those of interrupting the witness, the improved reduction in turn length is of about 10.25 words. The difference between the average length of a turn that uses semiconsecutive interpreting and

Table 4.4. Turn Length on Semiconsecutive Interpreting

Parameters	Constant	Turn Length	Interruptions
Estimated Parameters			
Estimated Coeficient	10.24673	−0.04501	−1.31831
T-Statistic	(7.13456)	(4.17227)	(7.07673)
Adjusted R-squared	0.12534		

the average length of a turn in which the interpreter relies on interrupting is approximately 11 words.[2] Since shorter segment lengths are associated with fewer errors of all types, I expected semiconsecutive interpreting to reduce total additions and omissions.

To test the costs or benefits of semiconsecutive interpreting, I examine the rate of additions and omissions on segmented data. First, I segment the data for utterances that are nine or fewer words, because semiconsecutive interpreting is observed, on average, at 8.9 words. The results for total additions and total omissions at this turn length are straightforward and indicate that the error rate for additions is not statistically significant ($t < 2.00$), as illustrated in Table 4.5. Table 4.5 shows that even though additions may be observed in the interpreters' renditions, they are random in occurrence. Hence, turn length plays no role in the errors that are made with nine or fewer words. This responds to the linguistic nature of semiconsecutive interpreting. When witnesses segment their output, they do so, on average, at appropriate grammatical junctures and at shorter turn lengths. Hence, the interpreter is less prone to make additions that may violate Grice's (1975) maxim of quantity. The results for total omissions, however, are significant and suggest a vast improvement when semiconsecutive interpreting is used in the courtroom. The rate of errors for omissions was about –0.33. These results indicate that for every 100 semiconsecutive events, there will be 33 fewer omissions.

Table 4.5. Total Additions and Total Omissions for Turn Lengths of Nine or Fewer Words

Total Additions			
Parameters	*Constant*	*Turn Length*	*Semiconsecutive*
Estimated Parameters			
Estimated Coeficient	0.02987	0.13230	0.03852
T-Statistic	(3.00162)	(15.41751)	(1.76901)
Adjusted R-squared	0.11015		
Total Omissions			
Parameters	*Constant*	*Turn Length*	*Semiconsecutive*
Estimated Parameters			
Estimated Coeficient	–0.61106	0.16922	–0.32903
T-Statistic	(3.10124)	(11.31345)	(–7.03344)
Adjusted R-squared	0.22142		

Table 4.6. Turn Lengths of Thirteen or More Words

Parameters	Constant	Turn Length	Semiconsecutive	Interruptions
Estimated Parameters				
Estimated Coeficient	0.30643	1.52577	–2.18774	3.59762
T-Statistic	(2.00115)	(–4.64233)	(–2.88935)	(2.06166)
Adjusted R-squared	0.14582			

Second, I compare the error rates of interruptions and semiconsecutive interpreting. I test the reduction in turn length and the error rate for additions and omissions at 13 or more words, because interruptions do not appear in the data until 22 words. The results show that at 13 or more words, semiconsecutive interpreting reduces turn length by approximately 2.2 words. Interruptions, on the other hand, add approximately 3.59 words to turn length. These results are reported on Table 4.6.

The error rate for total additions when interpreters use semiconsecutive interpreting and interruptions is not statistically significant, which indicates that turn length does not play a role in the error rates. Omissions, however, are significantly reduced with semiconsecutive interpreting by 1.2 words and significantly increased with interruptions by 0.86 words, as illustrated in Table 4.7.

Table 4.7. Total Additions and Total Omissions for Turn Lengths of Thirteen or More Words

Total Additions				
Parameters	Constant	Turn Length	Semiconsecutive	Interruptions
Estimated Parameters				
Estimated Coeficient	0.28101	0.17010	0.69966	–0.13230
T-Statistic	(5.67101)	(–5.49734)	(1.56084)	(–1.01326)
Adjusted R-squared	0.11228			
Total Omissions				
Parameters	Constant	Turn Length	Semiconsecutive	Interruptions
Estimated Parameters				
Estimated Coeficient	0.36562	0.01673	–1.20034	0.86730
T-Statistic	(3.19051)	(11.10682)	(–9.01344)	(–2.16326)
Adjusted R-squared	0.15734			

The findings presented in Table 4.7 suggest that semiconsecutive interpreting when compared with interruptions carries a net benefit rather than a net cost. Overall, semiconsecutive interpreting is better at reducing errors, particularly total omissions, because this mode of interpreting best addresses the issue of cognitive overload.

The practicality of using semiconsecutive interpreting in the courtroom, however, may be its most considerable limitation. Semiconsecutive interpreting depends on others for its execution. The interpreter may benefit from the technique, but is not the initiator. Thus, the interpreter does not have direct control of the use of semiconsecutive interpreting and must depend on others who may not be inclined to, or interested in, self-segmenting their output.

THE LIMITATIONS OF SEMICONSECUTIVE INTERPRETING: AN ISSUE OF POWER

One of the main complaints of the interpreters in my study, and the many with whom I have talked with throughout the years, is that expert witnesses and, in particular, attorneys do not often sufficiently consider their role and presence in the courtroom. Although none of the interpreters in the study expressed that the other members of the courtroom were responsible for the quality of their renditions, they were very much aware of who had power in the courtroom and the effect that power had over their working conditions.

My observations of courtroom interactions, coupled with the interpreters' comments, suggest that the manner in which the courtroom operates is not conducive to considering the difficulties associated with the interpreting process, particularly the issue of memory load. The courtroom is still a conservative, hierarchical, and patriarchal institution (Conley and O'Barr 1998; Mackinnon 1989) that serves best the efforts of those who have control over courtroom proceedings, rather than considering the legitimate needs of interpreters.

Interpreters are often expected to work in conditions that are not conducive to the reduction of negative environmental factors or cognitive overload. Vidal (1997) notes, for example, that judges and administrators often cite budgetary constrains when faced with interpreters' attempts to improve their working conditions. Many in the court system, specifically judges, also expect the interpreter to provide a literal and verbatim interpretation of legal proceedings (Mikkelson 1999; Minder 1989), without regard to the distinction between a literal and an accurate translation. It seems that the knowledge that has been accumulated about the interpreting process has not played a sufficiently important role in shaping the view of many in the legal profession. In essence, the interpreter is supposed to follow the lead of those who have power in the courtroom, specifically judges and attorneys, regardless of whether the path to be undertaken is smooth or filled with many bumps.

Attorneys traditionally have set the tone and complexity of courtroom discourse. They control what is asked and how it is asked. As Rigney (1997:124) discusses "turn allocation and turn type (i.e., question or answer) are predetermined, and who gets to talk in the courtroom, about what and when, is distributed according to social convention." Attorneys, thus, manage the conversational flow during the examination process, and witnesses are expected to respond to the attorneys' questions in a manner that is in tandem with the nature of the questions asked and what they intend to elucidate. In this study, the main determinant of whether an attorney asks a dense or lengthy question lies in whether he or she is performing a direct examination or cross-examination of a witness. The former often includes clear, concise, and fairly short questions:

(5) A: How many days was he in the hospital?
     I: ¿Cuántos dias estuvo él en el hospital?
     W: Llevaba como una semana.
     I: He had been there for about a week.
     A: And how was he responding to treatment?
     I: Y cómo estaba respondiendo al tratamiento?

From this line of examination, one perceives that the attorney does not want to overwhelm his or her own witness with too many details. A possible explanation for his strategy is to avoid an undesirable response that includes pauses, hesitations, or requests for clarification. With these types of questions, the interpreter is also able to provide a fairly accurate rendition. As with semiconsecutive interpreting, there is little textual density and the utterances are not voluminous. The opposite, however, is often observed when the attorney cross-examines a witness:

(6) A: Mrs. G in this case it was stipulated by the parties—by the person with the name I. D. A. under—under stipulated fact number seven on page five of the document, that prior to April 30th, 2001, new workers who were appointed as municipal transitory employees and paid from municipal funds were appointed to the following positions from March 16th through April 30th: worker, office clerk, secretary, and maintenance worker. Were you not aware of these positions? Did you qualify for any of these positions?
     (Sra. G en este caso las partes estipularon—por la persona de nombre I. D. A, bajo—bajo la evidencia estipulada número siete en la página cinco del documento, que antes de Abril 30 del 2001 los empleados nuevos que

fueron nombrados como empleados municiples transitorios y pagados por fondos municipales fueron nombrados a las siguientes posiciones de Marzo 16 a Abril 30: obrero, oficinista, secretaria, y empleado de mantenimiento. ¿No sabía usted de estas posiciones? ¿Cualificaba usted para alguna de estas posiciones?)

I: Las partes estipularon—por la persona de nombre I. D. A, bajo la evidencia estipulada en la página cinco del documento, que antes de Abril 30 del 2000—2001 los empleados nombrados como empleados transitorios y pagados, eh, por fondos municipales fueron nombrados de Marzo a Abril como trabajador, oficinista, empleado de mantenimiento. ¿Sabía usted de estas posiciones? ¿Cualificaba para alguna de ellas?

Here the attorney for the defense is engaged in a very contentious cross-examination of one of the plaintiffs, which is not atypical with this type of examination. In this example, the attorney is attempting to show the jury that the plaintiff is indeed aware of the new employment policies at the municipality. Counsel's strategy seems to be aimed at demonstrating that the reason for the municipality not rehiring the plaintiff is not because they are discriminating against her, as the plaintiff alleges, but rather because she does not qualify for any of the positions available. The attorney further wants to show that the plaintiff is aware that she does not qualify for any of the available job openings. The attorney's strategy, though it may have strengthened the defense's case, carried a cost for the interpreter. The discourse is dense and lengthy. The interpreter needs to recall a great deal of information, some of which is missed in her rendition. In this example, terms of address, dates, and lexical items are not recalled properly.

The examination of expert witnesses may also be dense or clear depending on whether the attorney is performing a direct or cross-examination of the witness. During direct examination, for example, the attorney's questions are often aimed at getting a narrative and easy-to-follow response from the expert witness:

(7) A: Could you explain to the jury the role of employment in the treatment of patients like Doña C?
    I: ¿Puede explicarle al jurado el papel que juega el trabajo en el tratamiento de pacientes como Doña C?
    W: Bueno, el tratamiento que yo inicié fue intensivo—
    (Well, the treatment that I initiated was intensive)
    I: Well, the treatment that I started with her was intensive—
    W: —Para que continuara adelante con su trabajo—
    (So she could go on with her job)
    I: And she could continue with her work—

W: —Logramos a través de la terápia ocupacional—
(We achieved through occupational therapy)
I: We achieved through this occupational therapy—
W: —Que la persona se motivara hasta cierto punto—
(That the person be motivated to a certain point)
I: That the person be motivated up to a point—
W: —Hacia el trabajo—
(Toward work)
I: Towards work.

As with other examples of semiconsecutive interpreting, the attorney's strategy did not carry a significant cost to the interpreter. When the same witness was cross-examined, however, the questions were aimed at challenging the witness's responses:

(8) A: And was she taking any medications for these conditions at that time?
   I: ¿En esos momento ella estaba tomando algun medicamento para estas condiciones?
   W: No recuerdo si ella estaba tomando, eh, medicación. Asumo que por la condición en que estaba ella, eh, estaba tomando medicamentos. Nosotros trabajamos intensivamente para tratar de, eh, de disminuir sus pensamientos negativos. En especial su pensamiento de suicida, porque encontraba que el mundo se le había prácticamente acabado en ese momento. Estaba muy deprimida.
   (I don't recall if she was taking, uh, medications. I assume that because of the condition in which she was, uh, she was taking medications. We worked intensely so as to, uh, to reduce her negative thoughts. Especially her suicidal thoughts, because she felt that her world was practically over at that time. She was very depressed)
   I: Well, I—I don't remember whether she was, but due to her condition I would presume that she was talking some medication. And we were working very hard to try to reduce her negative thoughts that—because at that time she was thinking that her world had come to an end.

This type of question requests a *yes* or *no* answer. As the example illustrates, the witness, who is testifying for the plaintiff, provides an explanation for his lack of certainty, and does not pause until he finishes his lengthy and elaborate response. His response seems to be aimed at explaining his understanding of the plaintiff's medical condition. The witness may have felt that the attorney was challenging his expertise, which results in the witness not relinquishing the conversational floor. In the data, expert witnesses whose knowledge of a subject was challenged often did not relinquish the conversational floor until they had had an opportunity to justify their past behavior or actions. The lack of self-segmentation in the witness's speech, unlike what is observed in example seven, carries a significant cost to the interpreter. The interpreter omits key aspects of the witness's testimony, such as hesitations and other linguistic content, that refer to the plaintiff's alleged suicidal thoughts and depression. This information is essential for the expert witness to demonstrate the severity of the plaintiff's condition, which presumably made it necessary for her to undergo aggressive therapy and take medication.

The attorney's strategy and the witness's level of response significantly affect whether the interpreter will be able to use semiconsecutive interpreting or even the consecutive mode at manageable levels. The cost to the quality of the interpreters' renditions is most evident during cross-examination, though it is also observed during direct examination. The question that arises, thus, is, whether changes can be implemented in the courtroom to give more power to the interpreter? One possibility, albeit not necessarily the easiest to implement in the courtroom, is to request that attorneys assume a more cooperative view of the examination process.

Attorneys could be made aware of the difficulties interpreters face in the courtroom and be requested to re-examine some of their trial tactics, mainly the length and complexity of their questions, so as not to interfere with the interpreters' ability to perform their duties well. This approach may improve the quality of the interpreters' renditions, but requires for its successful execution that the attorneys be willing to self-segment their output consistently. Attorneys, however, may not wish to always consider the presence of the interpreter in the courtroom. In fairness to the legal profession, semiconsecutive interpreting may not always reconcile well with what trial manuals recommend as the attorney's best examination strategy (Bailey and Rothblatt 1971).

Thus, the solution to the interpreters' diminished performance at higher turn lengths may not lie in expecting the attorneys to consistently self-segment their output. The most effective approach may be to create awareness in the legal profession about the potential benefits of semiconsecutive interpreting. The legal profession could use these findings to plan for the presence of the interpreter in the courtroom when developing their courtroom strategy. This approach, if found to be consistently beneficial, may increase the number of instances the legal profession is willing to consider the interpreters' limited processing ability, particularly when cross-examining witnesses.

The potential benefits of semiconsecutive interpreting also prompted me to draw analogies with other techniques that are under the control of the interpreter and that decrease memory load. As I will discuss in more detail in Chapter 5, the note taking technique, if implemented properly, could be used successfully in the bilingual courtroom to address the issue of taxed processing capacity. This technique has been studied in other settings in which interpreters use the consecutive mode, such as conference interpreting, and may also be

beneficial in courtroom interpreting, particularly if the effort to take notes includes those linguistic variables that seem to be most affected by turn length.

SUMMARY

In this chapter, I describe the linguistic and cognitive features of two length-
reducing strategies: interruptions and the semiconsecutive mode. Interpreters
in this study choose most often to interrupt the witness. These interruptions
are observed at either an inappropriate grammatical juncture or after the witness has provided a great deal of information. The former may lead to errors
because the interpreter chooses to interrupt at an inopportune time when he
or she expects more information from the speaker than he or she can handle.
The latter leads to errors, because the interpreter waits too long to interrupt.
The average length at which the interpreters in this study interrupt is 22
words. This results in about 0.3 errors per interrupted event.

For interruptions, the rate of errors is not statistically significant with total
additions. The results for total omissions, however, are significant and consistent with those findings on the effect of turn length reported in Chapter 3.
The results indicate that interpreters make 0.86 omissions per every interrupted turn of talk. This means that for every 100 interruptions, interpreters
will make 86 omissions. These omissions are the cost of the interpreters using interruptions as a means to reduce memory load. When these results are
examined next to those for the entire data (Chapter 3), they strongly suggest
that lack of recall is significantly affected in courtroom interpreting. From a
pragmatics perspective, this may translate to the witnesses' original utterances being rendered in a *powerful* style more often than a *powerless* style. In
the case of pragmatic markers, such as hesitations and the marker "well," this
may lead to a more favorable outcome for the witness.

Semiconsecutive interpreting, on the other hand, affects the source language discourse the least. This mode of interpreting reduces turn length by
1.3 words to an average length of 8.9 words. When these results are compared
with those of interrupting the witness, the improved reduction in turn length
is evident (10.25). The difference between the average length of a turn that
uses semiconsecutive interpreting and the average length of a turn in which
the interpreter relies on interrupting (21.75) is approximately 11 words. Since
shorter turn lengths are associated with fewer errors, the results for semiconsecutive interpreting show a reduction in errors in the courtroom, specifically
in omissions.

The error rate for total additions when interpreters use semiconsecutive interpreting and interruptions is not statistically significant, which indicates
randomness. Omissions, however, are significantly reduced with semiconsec-

utive interpreting. This is the net benefit of interpreters' using this strategy. When these results are compared with those of interruptions, semiconsecutive interpreting seems to be better at reducing errors, particularly total omissions, than interruptions. This mode of interpreting seems to address the issue of cognitive overload best and thus produces lower error rates.

Although interpreters' use of semiconsecutive interpreting seems to carry a net benefit, the practicality of using this strategy in the courtroom is limited. Semiconsecutive interpreting depends on other people for its execution. Although the interpreter may benefit from the technique, he or she is not the initiator. The interpreter does not have direct control over the use of semiconsecutive interpreting and, thus, must depend on others (i.e., attorneys and witnesses, who may not be inclined to self-segment their output). The result is a strategy that has its merits, but that cannot be consistently implemented in the courtroom. The analogies that can be drawn between our findings with semiconsecutive interpreting and other techniques that reduce memory load, such as note taking, are possibly one of the most significant contributions of this chapter.

The results of this study clearly point to the need to use techniques in the courtroom that the interpreter can control and that properly manage memory load. In Chapter 5, I will discuss the potential uses of the note taking technique in reducing errors triggered by increasing turn length.

NOTES

1. Recursion relates to the number of embedded sentences that can be strung together, which can be unlimited (Tallerman 2005:22).

2. The average length of interruptions minus the average length of a turn in the data: 21.75-10.25.

Chapter Five

On Using Note Taking Techniques in the Bilingual Courtroom

The findings on semiconsecutive interpreting suggest that court interpreters may benefit significantly from the use of techniques that properly manage memory load and that are in their direct control. In this chapter, I discuss how court interpreters may reduce memory load by embedding another activity such as note taking while performing their renditions.

Note-taking, although commonly used in conference interpreting, does not seem to have been fully embraced by the court-interpreting profession. The main complaint of court interpreters is that note taking takes too much processing effort and time from the task at hand. Although there is some legitimacy to these claims, the significant effect that memory load seems to have on the quality of the interpreters' renditions and potentially on the outcome of a trial should prompt the court interpreting profession to consider those skills that improve the interpreter's processing ability.

This chapter will include a discussion on the uses and, possible, limitations of the note taking technique, such as the issue of high processing effort, in consecutive interpreting. Furthermore, the chapter will address the potential benefits of the note taking technique in the bilingual courtroom and the need for future study and training in note taking.

GILE'S EFFORT MODEL OF CONSECUTIVE INTERPRETATION

The *Achilles heel*[1] of consecutive interpretation is cognitive overload. Interpreters who perform in the consecutive mode must often wait long intervals between the time they receive input and the time they produce output. The result of this linguistic "wait" may be evidenced in the deterioration of the interpreter's performance. The root cause of much of this deterioration lies in the processing and capacity limitations of short-term memory (STM), which is key to the interpreting process.

Input enters STM as a result of attention to acoustic or visual stimuli. Once input enters STM, it is retained only for a short period of time (Atkinson and Shiffrin 1968; Smith 1985). Unlike long-term memory (LTM) neural mechanisms are not created for later recall in STM (Peterson 1959). For input to be retained in STM, it needs to be encoded at an acoustic (Matthei and Roper 1985), visual (Posner and Keele 1967), or semantic (Baddeley 1966, 1990) level. If the input is not properly encoded and/or too much information is received at once (Baddeley et al. 1975), the information is lost and cannot be stored in LTM for later retrieval.

Researchers (Gile 1995; Kade and Cartellieri 1971; Moser 1978) who study the cognitive aspects of interpreting recognize the relationship between a decline in output and increased demands on the interpreters STM. Gile (1995), for example, developed the *Effort Models* of interpreting to help interpreters who work in both the simultaneous and consecutive mode to understand the difficulties of the interpreting process and to assist them in selecting strategies that improve the quality of their renditions.

The *Effort Model* of consecutive interpreting is divided in two phases. Phase one of consecutive interpreting includes the listening and note taking phase and the speech production phase:

Interpretation = L + N + M + C
     L   Listening and analysis
     N   Note-taking
     M   Short-term Memory Operations
     C   Coordination

The listening and analysis effort consists of all comprehension-oriented operations, such as the interpreter's analysis of sound waves from the source language to the identification and meaning-recognition of words in the source language. The memory effort in consecutive interpreting is linked to the taking or, alternatively, non-taking of notes.

Phase two of consecutive interpreting includes the following components:

Interpretation = Rem + Read + P
     Rem Remembering
     Read Note-Reading
     P   Production

The remembering component refers to the effort interpreters devote to recalling the source-language discourse. Gile notes that this component is different from the short-term memory one, because long-term memory operations are at play in the second phase of consecutive interpreting. The *Read* component refers to the reading of notes, which may assist in the remembering process. As Gile (1995) explains if the interpreter takes good notes they should help him or her perform *Rem* operations and reduce the amount of information that needs to be recalled from memory.

The production effort is the last stage of consecutive interpreting. In the production stage of interpreting is where speech production failures are observed. These problems are often evident in the interpreter's use of speech disfluencies and hesitations, which may signal difficulties when searching for lexical or syntactic equivalencies. Production failures seem to be related to the interpreting process itself, which differs from free and fluent speech, and on the interpreter's approach to reconstructing the speech from source to target language.

The use of notes during consecutive interpreting may reduce saturation and production errors. For note taking to be effective, however, researchers and practitioners must address both the possible limitations of this technique and also the choice of language and code for note taking. In the context of the bilingual courtroom, choice of language and type of information noted is important, because it may be significantly related to the quality of the interpreter's renditions.

THE EFFECTIVENESS OF NOTE TAKING IN CONSECUTIVE INTERPRETING

One of the most important questions to ask on the effectiveness of note taking in consecutive interpreting is whether note taking substantially improves recall. Although there are no empirical studies that can provide a definite answer to this question, success in note taking seems to be related to language choice, to economy of mental and hand effort, and to the skill of the interpreter.

The issue of whether interpreters should take notes in the target language or source language, for example, has been heavily debated. Most of the research is based on personal observations rather than empirical testing, which have added to the controversy. On the non-empirical side there are some researchers such as Matyssek (1989) who have argued that if interpreters chose to take notes using language, rather than code, the mother tongue should be the preferred choice for note taking. Matyssek bases his arguments on the notion that interpreters have superior mastery of their mother tongue, which should translate into better notes. Aside from Matyssek, who proposes the use of the interpreter's mother tongue, most authors advocate for the use of either the target language (Mikkelson 1993; Rozan 1956; Seleskovitch 1975) or source language (Alexieva 1993; Gile 1995).

Those who advocate for the use of the target language argue that interpreters who take notes in the target language focus on the surface form of the input, which should result in superior processing of the input. This group also argues that taking notes in the target language should assist in the production of the target speech because conversion has already taken place.

The arguments of those who question the use of the target language lie in the fact that note taking in the target language may require more processing capacity. The interpreter must mentally transform the incoming speech into the target language before he or she can take notes. This process is thought to increase the number of operations the interpreter must perform during the listening phase. The listening phase of consecutive interpreting appears to be more capacity consuming than the production phase and, if taxed with the reformulation of notes, may be significantly affected.

On the empirical side of note taking research, Dam's (2004) study provides some promising results. Dam studied the notes of four subjects who were studying for a European Masters in Conference Interpreting at the Copenhagen Business School in Denmark. The students, during a classroom session, were asked to interpret a Spanish source text consecutively into Danish (task 1) and a Danish source text into Spanish (task 2). The students' training in note taking was uniform, and it was based on the principles proposed by Rozan (1956). The individual nature of note taking, however, had been stressed during the term of the course. The students were not instructed to take notes in any particular language, still they were told to take notes in "whichever language came to their mind when listening to the source speech" (Dam 2004:7). Three of the subjects were native Danish speakers (*A-language*) and had Spanish as a foreign language (*B-language*). The fourth subject had Spanish as a native language. Dam's findings, although from a small data set, are intriguing:

> Generally speaking, the choice of language in note-taking seems to be governed mainly by the status of the language in the interpreter's language combination, i.e. whether it is an A- or a B-language, and much less by the status in the task, i.e. whether it is the source or the target language (2004:12).

These findings, as Dam notes, seem to support those of Matyssek (1989). The interpreters in her study seem partial to taking notes in their native language (*A-language*), possibly because it minimizes efforts. Dam remarks that interpreters are prone to take notes in the language that is easiest and fastest. The native language may fit this requirement best, particularly as compared with a foreign language. She notes, however, that there may be benefits to using the source language for note taking, because the interpreter can write down what he or she hears. Dam does not recommend taking notes in the target language, because "language conversion or simultaneous activation of two languages becomes an additional requirement" (2004:13).

Dam's findings on note taking seem to suggest that note taking in the native or source language are superior choices to taking notes in a foreign language or in the target language. These findings, albeit promising, need to be tested further. Her data set is small and does not include professional interpreters working in an authentic setting. The results, thus, may not be representative of the choices that consecutive interpreters make when performing in actual working conditions.

The skill of the interpreter may also be an important measure of success in note taking. Gile (1990), for example, observed in his experiments with students that the benefits of note taking need to be measured with interpreters who are trained and have acquired the skill of note taking. In this view, if the note taker is not properly trained or does not use the most effective note-taking techniques, the product of the interpreter's efforts will be diminished or lost.

The final question that seems to concern researchers who study note taking is whether to use language or symbols when taking notes. Alexieva (1993:203) mentions that the guiding principle for choice of code should be what carries *maximum economy*. She advises that the choice of code should consider the time used for taking notes, the manual effort to take down the notes, and the clarity of the symbols to be interpreted. Symbols that are too general, for example, do not carry enough semantic information to be useful. For Alexieva (2003:203), notes that activate semantic networks are particularly useful, because they can be economical while enhancing the interpreter's ability to make inferences and produce quality renditions.

For other researchers, such as Gile (1995) and Dam (2004), note taking can be performed either verbatim or using words. As Gile (1995:181) explains, "note-taking is not governed by rules of linguistic acceptability—lexical, syntactic, stylistic, or otherwise...notes can be taken with much latitude." The author adds, however, that if an interpreter chooses to use symbols and abbreviations, they need to be mastered by the interpreter prior to use so as to reduce the capacity-consuming effects of note taking.

Regardless of the code or language the interpreter chooses to use for his or her renditions, the consensus among the majority of authors in the field of consecutive interpreting is that note taking needs to be structured and economical, that is, notes should not be taken for everything, and should contribute to the interpreter's better recall of the original. Although much empirical evidence is still needed to establish which note-taking strategy is best at reducing processing capacity, prior research and observational studies seem to indicate that note taking in consecutive interpreting may carry significant benefits for its users. These benefits should be considered more seriously in the bilingual courtroom. The following sections will address the possible uses of note taking in courtroom interpreting and the need for future research in the field.

NOTE TAKING IN THE BILINGUAL COURTROOM: POSSIBLE USES AND APPLICATIONS

The pedagogical implications of prior research in the training of courtroom interpreters point to the need to create awareness about the concept of processing capacity. Those who are studying interpreting need to be shown the differences between listening, analyzing, and producing speech for interpreting and for every day life. This appears to be the logical starting point to introducing exercises in note taking and the *Effort Models* of consecutive interpreting.

In the case of experienced courtroom interpreters, such as those in this study, this initial step may not need to be overtly demonstrated. Courtroom interpreters, in general, seem to be aware of the great deal of mental effort that their work requires. The problem seems to lie, however, in their failure to recognize fully the connection between the effects of interpreting on memory load and the need to train in techniques that may unburden their processing capacity, specifically the use of notes. Although some researchers and practitioners[2] are involved in the training of note taking for courtroom interpreters, more needs to be done to establish a connection between improved performance and note taking. I will attempt to provide some suggestions based on the adaptation of prior experiments with students (Gile 1995) that could be used to introduce exercises in note taking (Gillies 2005; Rozan 1956) with courtroom interpreters.

TRAINING SUGGESTIONS: A LOOK AT A GROUP OF COURTROOM INTERPRETERS

A training session for courtroom interpreters could be designed to demonstrate the potential benefits of note taking in the bilingual courtroom. This session shares some similarities with Gile's (1995) training session with students, but with some important variations that account for the findings of this book and those of prior research on the bilingual courtroom. The focus here is on examining the interpreters' recall of pragmatic and extralinguistic content rather than names. Interpreters often seem to recall poorly linguistic variables that provide tone and style to the original.

In this task, I asked five court-certified interpreters (3 female and 2 male) who work in the Atlanta, Georgia metropolitan area to participate in a note-taking exercise. These interpreters were attending a training seminar on legal terminology (Spanish/English) and volunteered to participate in the exercise. None of the interpreters had received formal training in note taking, though two of them remarked that they occasionally took simple notes to assist in the recall of names and numbers. The interpreters were divided into two groups. One group (*Group A*), which was comprised of two interpreters, was instructed not to take notes and the other group (*Group B*), which was comprised of the remaining three interpreters, was instructed to take notes. Those who took notes were told that they could take notes using either words or code, whichever was most economical. They were also told that they could use whichever language they preferred (i.e., source, native, target, or foreign language). Interestingly, those in the note-taking group remarked that they would prefer to use the source language, because they believed it to be easier. After the initial instructions were provided, the training instructor was asked to read an utterance from an actual trial. The texts were lengthy, as it is often the case in the courtroom, and included the linguistic features that have been found most often to be omitted or rendered improperly in the bilingual courtroom, such as politeness markers, terms of address, and speech disfluencies. These linguistic variables, which assign tone and style, were discussed and defined prior to the exercise. The following is an actual example used for the exercise. A total of five turns of talk were used:

(1) *Mr. Jones, uh*, you mentioned that the marketing of the product was not your responsibility. You say *sir* that there was a sales meeting on Friday that you did not attend. You allege that Mr. Smith, *uh, did— did* not inform you about the sales meeting on Friday. Could you *please* tell us if any of the other area supervisors were informed of this meeting?

After the instructor reaches the end of a turn of talk, each interpreter in the group was asked to provide individually a rendition of the linguistic markers tested, specifically terms of address, politeness, and speech disfluencies. The interpreters' renditions were recorded and transcribed. The number of linguistic markers each group heard was compared. The results of the exercise for all five turns of talk are summarized in Table 5.1.

These results show that, on average, those interpreters who took notes (*Group B*) are able to recall more of the linguistic variables than those interpreters who did not take notes (*Group A*). The interpreters who took notes, for example, have better recall of two pragmatic markers: "terms of address" and

Table 5.1.   Recall of Linguistic Variables

Variable	Terms of Address	Politeness	"Well"	S. Disfluency
Group				
Group A	12	7	10	0
Group B	15	3	12	0
Total	27	10	22	0
Total Variables	(32)	(15)	(26)	(15)

"well." The interpreters who did not take notes, however, are able to recall politeness markers at a much higher rate (70% *vs.* 30%). This is the only linguistic marker that exhibits this variation. Neither group of interpreters is able to recall all of the linguistic variables (*Total Variables*). The rate of recall for total linguistic variables is less than 50% for each group and for each linguistic variable tested. This indicates an improvement from not taking notes, but also suggests that there are still cognitive and/or linguistic factors, such as turn length, that are not entirely addressed by note taking. The use of notes does not improve either the recollection of pauses, such as "uh," or other speech disfluencies, such as hesitations or false starts. This is an important finding, because it seems to be consistent with the notion that courtroom interpreters view these types of linguistic variables as meaningless (Hale 2002) and, hence, omit them consistently, particularly at higher turn lengths (Chapter 3).

In addition to examining the rate of recall for each linguistic variable, I also examined whether note taking assisted in the recall of onset-initial linguistic variables. In this study, the position of a linguistic variable in an utterance seems to play a significant role in its recollection as shown in Table 5.2. In the data, I do not observe any instances of onset-initial politeness markers; hence they are not tested. The results of this exercise suggest that taking notes assists in the overall recall of onset-initial "terms of address" and, the onset-initial discourse marker "well." The rate of recall for total onset-initial linguistic variables, however, is less than 50% for each group and for each linguistic variable tested. Moreover, the use of note taking does not improve the recollection of onset-initial speech disfluencies. As in Table 5.1, the interpreters who perform the task are not able to recall speech disfluencies regardless of the position of the linguistic variable in the utterance or whether they took notes.

The findings of this exercise, with a small number of courtroom interpreters, provide some preliminary evidence in favor of the use of note taking in the courtroom. The interpreters' overall recall of some linguistic variables, such as "terms of address" and the marker "well," for example, seems to have

Table 5.2. Recall of Onset-Initial Linguistic Variables

Variable	Terms of Address	"Well"	S. Disfluency
Group			
Group A	6	9	0
Group B	9	11	0
Total	15	20	0
Total Variables	(25)	(26)	(10)

improved when they used notes. These results, however, are not scientific. Further study needs to be performed with a larger sample of courtroom interpreters so as to determine whether the use of note taking in the courtroom reduces significantly interpreter-induced errors. One question, in particular, that needs to be addressed is whether being formally trained in note taking reduces court interpreters' additions and omissions of the linguistic variables discussed in this work (see Chapter 3). The answer to this question is important, because interpreters are expected to maintain the tone, style, and intent of the original, and note taking may improve their ability to do so. A larger and empirically sound analysis of note taking in the bilingual courtroom would provide the interpreting community with evidence against or in favor of the use of note taking in the courtroom. In the next sections, I will provide some training suggestions in note taking for courtroom interpreters and a plan for future empirical research in the field.

NOTE TAKING FOR COURTROOM INTERPRETERS: SOME SUGGESTIONS

The findings of my exercise with courtroom interpreters suggest that taking notes improves interpreters' recollection of key linguistic variables. The extent to which interpreters are able to recall linguistic content may depend on whether they have received training prior to taking notes. As Rozan (1956) argues, the real work of consecutive interpreting must be done before the interpreter starts to read back his or her notes. Although there is not just one approach to note taking, and interpreters may vary in their use of notes, it seems that there are significant similarities among most, if not all, note-taking styles (Gillies 2005).

One approach to effective note taking in consecutive interpreting includes having the interpreters take vertical-style notes of key linguistic features after listening to an actual text from a trial, such as that illustrated in example 1. The notes should assist the interpreter in making connections as to the position in which linguistic content appears in the utterance and their role in assigning pragmatic and semantic content. As Gillies (2005) proposes the interpreter should proceed as follows:

- Note the underlying meaning and not the word used
- Separate ideas on the page
- Note vertically
- Use diagonal notation
- Use links and symbols
- Have consistent rules for abbreviation

The first rule has to do with economy and is self-explanatory. The next rule has to do with grouping ideas. The method Gillies recommends, based on Rozan's (1956) work, is to note linguistic content in a manner equivalent to a sentence (subject-verb-object) and divide each group on the page with a horizontal line. If the interpreter were to render an utterance such as "John was attending a meeting in the Balkans. The meeting signaled an important point in the development of his new business venture," the notes may look similar to example 2. The horizontal line would mark the end of the first section and beginning of the next one. It is important to note that the degree of detail in the note-taking process may vary among courtroom interpreters and, for expediency sake, may not need to be as detailed, as in the above example.

(2)   John

                  attending

                              meeting

_____

        meeting

              signal

                    development

                              (new) business

The interpreter is encouraged to note vertically also, from top to bottom on the page, and each subsequent element should be noted below and to the right of the previous one. The idea behind this style of note taking is that the interpreter focuses on "who is doing what to whom." After this concept is mastered, the interpreter can work on the details. At this stage, links, symbols, and abbreviations can also be incorporated, as long as they are clear, are time-saving, and are used consistently.

In the context of the bilingual courtroom some additional note taking may be required, as it is illustrated in the example in example 3. In this example, the notes serve to mark the key linguistic features of the passage, and the interpreter may be given some liberty as to how much information needs to be included in the text, particularly as it regards the notation of pragmatic content. The interpreter, for example, after receiving instruction in the basic principles of note taking (Example 1), could be instructed to consider pragmatic content, such as the politeness marker "sir." The latter is one of the linguistic variables most often omitted in the bilingual courtroom and may require special attention. The interpreter could also receive formal training in the use of simple codes or symbols to note extralinguistic content. Codes or symbols could be used to mark that a repetition or repair sequence follows or that multiple hesitations were made. The interpreter could use brackets with numbers, such as [1], or an asterisk [*], as in example 3, to mark that they heard a speech disfluency at a certain point in an utterance.

(3)   A: Uh— uh, the man that you say, sir, attacked you, uh, was he a member of the police department?
Notes:

[*] man

you

say (sir)

attacked[*]

The use of codes or symbols to note stylistic and pragmatic content, however, should not take away from the note-taking process itself. The main purpose of note taking is to improve interpreters' overall recall of the source language. The notation of style and register is, thus, only intended to facilitate interpreters' recall of relevant pragmatic information, but without sacrificing other linguistic content. Future study, however, is needed to gather more substantial and significant evidence of the benefits of note taking in the bilingual courtroom. In the next section, I will discuss some possible directions for future research.

NOTE TAKING IN THE BILINGUAL
COURTROOM: THE NEED FOR FUTURE STUDY

The ideal research scenario for the study of note taking in the bilingual court-room would include a large set of data produced by a representative selection of randomly selected courtroom interpreters working in an authentic setting. This scenario, although ideal, carries many limitations. One of the most significant ones is the lack of courtroom interpreters who take notes. As I discussed in Chapter 2, the interpreters in my study remarked that they hardly took notes, if ever. The latter seems to be the norm for a large portion of the court interpreting profession. The consensus among the interpreters in this work, for example, was that note taking took too much time and reduced their ability to store large chunks of information into memory. The lack of authentic data, thus, points to the need to perform controlled studies. I will suggest the methodology to perform a study that examines the potential costs and benefits of using note taking in the courtroom.

The controlled study should consist of a mock trial. The data for the trial should consist of an actual case that is used for all interpreting events. The length of the trial should be less than 30 minutes, to minimize the effect of fatigue (Moser-Mercer et al. 1998) in the study. The location of the mock trial should be the same for all interpreters, so as to control environmental factors such as audio quality (Gerver 1974) and setting. The actors who play the roles of witnesses and attorneys should be of the same gender and, ideally, the same cultural and educational background as the individuals in the actual trial. The interpreters should be divided into groups. Each group should have approximately 30 members so as to avoid small sample problems and enhance the robustness of the data.

The first group of interpreters will be instructed not to take notes while performing their renditions. The second group will have received formal training in note taking and will be instructed to take notes while performing their renditions. The interpreter's training in note taking will be largely based on the principles proposed by Rozan (1956) and Gillies (2005), which are outlined in this chapter. The third group, which is optional, will have had practice in note taking, but will not have received any formal training in the technique. This group will take notes during the study and will serve as a control group to help establish whether formal training improves the interpreters' renditions as opposed to idiosyncratic "learning by doing." A fourth and fifth set of groups could also be created to test whether those interpreters who take notes in the source or native language perform more accurate renditions than those who take notes in the target or foreign language.

Once the groups have been selected at random, each interpreter in the group will perform their renditions individually and in isolation, so as not to influence the other interpreters in the study. The researcher should also consider not providing the interpreters with too much information about the case or about the actors. Interpreters may form preconceived notions about the witnesses, which may affect the types of notes they take and how much information is noted.

The study will produce a data set that can be interpreted on different levels. The basic statistics consist of a difference in means test. For each linguistic variable, the mean rate of errors (additions, omissions, and changes) will be calculated along with their standard deviations. A simple formula will be applied to determine whether the means for each of the error rates are significantly different from the others.

Another more informative approach would include a regression analysis of the data. Regressing the linguistic variables on turn lengths and on a constant will tell us the relationship between turn length and a particular addition or omission, and whether the constant is significant. The estimated coefficients on turn length, as discussed in previous chapters, will have associated standard errors. From these, the researcher can determine whether one group's error rate is significantly different from another's. The information generated by linear regressions, for example, would tell us whether the group that used the note-taking technique improved, or diminished, the rate of errors for the linguistic variables tested and at higher turn lengths.

The information generated by linear regressions or the difference in means test may prove useful for training purposes. The results of the statistical analysis, particularly if they prove that the note-taking technique is beneficial, may be used by the legal interpreting community and those who provide training to increase awareness of the benefits of note taking in the courtroom. Increased awareness may prompt more courtroom interpreters to train in the use of note taking and embrace the use of notes while performing their renditions. The interpreters' response to the results of my exercise and to an empirically sound study may result in an overall reduction of errors, such as those that affect the tone, style, and intent of the original.

SUMMARY

Although note taking seems to be commonly used in other venues that use consecutive interpreting, such as conference interpreting, court interpreters have not fully embraced the use of notes when providing renditions in the courtroom. In this chapter, I propose that the court interpreting community should examine more closely the possible benefits of note taking given its potential uses as a memory reinforcer.

The findings presented in Chapters 3 and 4 point to a significant relationship between increasing turn length and the linguistic variables that seem to affect the most the pragmatic and semantic properties of the original, particularly those that may sway jurors' opinions of witnesses and attorneys. Interpreting, even in the best of scenarios, takes up a great deal of mental effort. As turn length increases, the interpreter's performance seems to deteriorate significantly. Note taking, if performed correctly, may act as an effective memory reinforcer and assist the court interpreter in having better recall of the original.

In an informal exercise, I asked five court-certified interpreters (3 female and 2 male) who work in the Atlanta, Georgia metropolitan area to participate in a note-taking exercise. One group (*Group A*) was asked not to take notes, and the other group (*Group B*) was asked to do so. The interpreters had not received any formal training in note taking prior to the exercise. The results of this exercise suggest that those interpreters who took notes were able to recall linguistic variables, such as *term of address* and the discourse marker *well*, better than those interpreters who did not take notes. The interpreters who did not take notes, however, had better recall of politeness markers. Neither group was able to recall speech disfluencies. This points to the possible "meaningless" status of these stylistic variables, which interferes with their encoding. The recall of onset-initial variables was also improved with the group that took notes, except for onset-initial speech disfluencies. Neither group of interpreters was able to recall this type of stylistic marker.

The results of the informal exercise, although intriguing, are not scientific. The future of note taking as an effective strategy to reduce errors in the bilingual courtroom, depends on the findings of future empirical research. Researchers who specialize in the field should conduct controlled-studies that provide significant empirical evidence on the potential benefits or costs of note taking. This chapter provides the methodological foundation for some of this research. The results of these studies, particularly if they prove that note taking is beneficial in the courtroom, may prompt the legal interpreting community to embrace the teaching of note taking and to apply it consistently in the courtroom.

NOTES

1. This term was used by De Groot (1997:27) to describe the difficulties of the consecutive mode of interpreting.

2. Holly Mikkelson, who is a professor of interpreting at the Monterrey Institute of International Studies, Monterrey, California, is actively involved in the training of courtroom interpreters (www.acebo.com).

Chapter Six

Gender Differences in the Management of Cognitive Overload

Prior studies on language and the law (O'Barr 1982; O'Barr and Atkins 1980) have suggested that gender is not significantly correlated with the use of *powerless* speech in the courtroom. In this chapter, I will examine whether cognitive overload, coupled with sociolinguistic factors, may help explain the relationship between an interpreter's gender and his or her addition and omission of key linguistic variables from the original. The findings of this study, particularly if I find a relationship between interpreter-induced errors and an interpreter's gender, could be used as a basis for future research and also as a means to address during training the potential differences between male and female interpreters.

THE LINGUISTIC STUDY OF GENDER

Robin Lakoff's (1975) seminal work *Language and Woman's Place* set the stage for a great deal of linguistic research on language and gender. In her book, Lakoff argues that society expects a woman to "talk like a lady." The linguistic features that she identifies as "women's language" are those that soften women's self-expression:

- Tag questions ("you went to the store, didn't you")
- Hedges ("that's sorta interesting")
- Precise color terms ("mauve" instead of "purple")
- Indirection ("well, she is smart")
- Conventional politeness ("would you please close the door")

Lakoff associates these linguistic forms with a women's sense of powerlessness. Women use powerless speech because they avoid assuming positions of authority and they are afraid to show strong commitment and opinions. The lack of assertiveness in women's speech has a cost, because it often translates into a lack of effectiveness when trying to get others to do their biding.

Although, Lakoff's findings directed attention to the study of gendered speech, they were met with a great deal of skepticism and debate. The author did not gather any quantitative data to support her claims and, for the most part, based her findings on her own language use and those of acquaintances. These criticisms, thus, led the way for future research that challenges or attempts to better explain Lakoff's claims. The work of O'Barr and Atkins (1980) is one of the first to examine whether a speaker's gender plays a significant role in determining the use of *powerless* speech in the context of the courtroom.

O'Barr and Atkins (1980) find that the strongest determinant of a witness's use of a particular testimony style, such as a *powerless* or *powerful* speech style, is the witness's social status and familiarity with the courtroom rather than his or her gender. In O'Barr and Atkin's study, people of low socioeconomic background and people with no previous experience in the courtroom most often use *powerless* speech styles.

Other researchers (Tannen 1990 and Holmes 1998) have suggested that power inequities may arise from cultural differences and from the manner in which men and women are socialized. The cultural view of gendered speech proposes that the way men and women interact from an early age sets their speech patterns later on. Hence, women learn at an early age to aim for intimacy and rapport building, whereas men aim for status and independence. Tannen (1990) remarks that "the chief commodity that is bartered in the boy's hierarchical world is status…the chief commodity that is bartered in the girl's community is intimacy" (47).

In this view, because boys and girls are socialized differently they develop different sub-cultures with different sets of norms for conversational interaction. Conversational interactions between men and women are, thus, defined as a form of cross-cultural communication. Women, on the one hand, lean towards communicative behavior that is supportive and context-sensitive as a means to focus and enhance solidarity. Men, on the other hand, use language in a manner that is unsupportive, that concedes little to the addressee, and that secures power and enhances status (Holmes 1998).

The communicative differences observed between the sexes, thus, lie, in how men and women have been shaped by their culture and social environment. As Holmes (1998:477) remarks "men are the power brokers in most speech communities. Women are subordinate. Consequently, the patterns of interaction which distinguish the sexes reflect male dominance and female subordination." To this statement I will add that context is essential to support this notion. That is, women may be socialized to speak differently than men, but the context in which a communicative exchange takes place may enhance or diminish power differences between the sexes.

In the context of the courtroom, attorneys and judges, regardless of their gender, are in positions of authority. In the case of my data, I found female attorneys to be even more aggressive linguistically than the men, particularly during cross-examination. The sense of power that attorneys and judges have, however, is not passed down to the interpreters. Interpreters are expected to be invisible and non-intrusive. This expectation of invisibility extends to their renditions. Interpreters are expected to maintain the tone and style of the original despite their innate abilities, socialization, and cultural background. In essence, the interpreters's role in the courtroom demands that they overcome the possible trappings of their gender, socialization, and even cognitive biology.

COGNITIVE FUNCTIONING, LINGUISTIC SKILLS, AND GENDER

Studies (Bouma 1990; Chambers 1992; Meyers-Levy 1994, 1989) that have examined the relationship between gender and linguistic skills have shown that left-hemisphere dependence observed in females makes them more likely to use verbal strategies to process information. Verbal ability is primarily a left hemisphere function and may account for females' superiority in verbal tasks. Chambers (1992), for example, links females' apparent genetic and neurological advantages to the development of sociolinguistic and verbal skills:

> There is, in the psychological literature, a long record of evidence of female verbal superiority. Over many years, women have demonstrated an advantage over men in tests of fluency, speaking, sentence complexity, analogy, listening, comprehension of both written and spoken material, vocabulary and spelling (1992:199).

Although Chambers notes that there is only a slight biological advantage for women, this advantage may be sufficient for women to build on their language skills and develop them further.

Women's advantage in verbal skills is also observed in studies that examine verbal recall. Women, for example, outperform men in a variety of recall tasks such as those that involve the learning and recalling of items from a list

(Bridge et al. 2006; Herlitz et al. 1997; Maitland et al. 2004; Yonker et al. 2003), those that involve recall of stories (Bridge et al. 2006; Persinger and Richards 1995; Hultsch et al. 1991), and those that involve recall of verbal episodic memory tasks (Bridge et al. 2006; Kimura and Clarke 2002; Herlitz et al. 1999, 1997). The findings of these studies share many similarities because women appear more successful than men in retrieving detailed information from memory during exercises that require the verbal recollection of past experiences or events.

In studies that involve the recall of stories, for example, Bridge and her colleagues (2006) found that "women not only recalled more words from a narrative than men did, but they were also able to reconstruct the story better, by recalling more correct themes and ideas" (2006:35). It seems that because item-to-context binding is necessary for successful retrieval, women may be able to recall more items from a narrative because of their tendency to link specific items to a structured context.

Studies on verbal recall also suggest that women's superior performance may be due to the role socialization may play in encoding and recalling information. Studies that have investigated the recall of emotionally linked events, for example, have found differences between the genders that may be socially based. In the case of autobiographical events, such as childhood memories, women were found to have superior recall to men. Childhood memories are often linked to emotional experiences that have a positive or negative impact on the individual (Friedman and Pines 1991). Other studies with children also show that girls have an advantage when it comes to recalling emotion-related events. Buckner and Fivush (1998), for example, find that girls recall more interpersonal experiences that are linked to the self. Colley and her colleagues (2002) propose that the findings of prior research point to the relationship between socialization, gender, and recall. They argue that "such findings are strongly suggestive of more efficient encoding of person- and emotion-related information by girls, perhaps as a result of their socialization into person-oriented and communal gender role" (577-78).

It is important to note that although women outperform men in a variety of recall tasks, men and women show different degrees of success when encoding and recalling same-gender cues. In Crawford and English's (1994) study, for example, men and women are presented with essays in which the target is described using a generic term, such as "he/male," or a specific term that specifically includes women, such as "he/she." They find that men recall more content when the generic referent is used, whereas women have better recall when the gender-inclusive term is used. In this study, men and women appear to have different responses to tasks that are associated with masculine or female gender roles. Recall, thus, seems to be influenced by differences in interpretation based on perceived relevance. In the context of the courtroom, the interpreters' gender may also influence their addition and omission of linguistic variables from their renditions.

GENDER AND TURN LENGTH:
SIMILARITIES OR DIFFERENCES

The first task of this analysis is to examine whether the interpreter's gender plays a role in the rates of additions and omissions observed in the data. To estimate this relationship, I use a regression analysis that is consistent with that used for semiconsecutive interpreting and interruptions. In this estimation, gender[1] and turn length are treated as independent variables. The results of this analysis are reported in Table 6.1. The regression results show that gender does not seem to play a significant role in causing errors. This is reflected by the *t*-statistic, which is not statistically significant ($t < 2.0$) for gender. These results indicate that women, on average, do not make more errors than men when performing their renditions. The manner in which male and female interpreters manage cognitive overload, however, may cause the interpreters to make different types of errors. In the next section, I will address the possible role of socialization in explaining the differences between male and female interpreters' processing of linguistic information at high memory load.

GENDER DIFFERENCES IN COURTROOM INTERPRETING:
THE FEMALE INTERPRETER'S PERSPECTIVE

The study of gender in both linguistics and psychology suggests that when it comes to language use, verbal skills, and memory performance, men and women exhibit significant differences. In the context of courtroom interpreting, I also find gender to be a factor in the types of errors observed in the data.

Table 6.1.   The Relationship between Gender and Rate of Errors for Total Events

	Parameters	Constant	Turn Length	Gender
Estimated Parameters				
Estimated Coefficient		(-0.36118)	–0.73520	0.09586
T-Statistic		(2.76001)	(-5.65839)	(0.98269)
Adjusted R-squared	0.37923			

Male and female interpreters in this study treat some linguistic variables differently as the length of a turn increases. The results of the estimations, for example, suggest that the error rates for omissions of terms of address and for the addition of politeness markers are significant for women and not for men, as Table 6.2 shows. The differences in error rates (estimated coefficient) and the difference in significance (*t*-statistic) for male and female interpreters suggest that the gender of the interpreter plays a role in how specific linguistic variables are treated as turn length increases. Female interpreters, for example, seem to be more prone to omit those linguistic features that signal deference (Brown and Levinson 1987; Fraser 2005; Goffman 1967). As turn length increases, female interpreters seem also more prone to add those linguistic features that signal politeness, such as "please" and "thank you." In both cases, the interpreters seem to omit or add information for which they have been socialized to either reject or value.

FEMALE INTERPRETERS' TREATMENT OF DEFERENCE

Fraser (2005:69) notes that deference is marked by the situation. Thus, one would expect that a setting such as the courtroom would inspire some sense of deference for its members, for the process itself, and for those who rely on the system for justice. The interpreters in this study, regardless of their gender, communicated to me that they were very much aware of the formality of

Table 6.2.   The Relationship between Gender and Rate of Errors:
Terms of Address and Politeness Markers

	Terms of Address Omitted		
	Parameters	*Male*	*Female*
Estimated Parameters			
Estimated Coefficient		0.01652	1.04321
T-Statistic		(0.16389)	(2.76551)
Adjusted R-squared	0.24581		
	Politeness Markers Added		
	Parameters	*Male*	*Female*
Estimated Parameters			
Estimated Coefficient		0.03988	0.21138
T-Statistic		(1.16432)	(3.34960)
Adjusted R-squared	0.27002		

the courtroom and of the importance to maintain in their renditions those linguistic features that marked deference in the original. The male interpreters' treatment of deference is consistent with their views of the formality of the courtroom and of their role in the trial process. The female interpreters' treatment (IF) of the same linguistic features, however, was not:

(1) A: Ma'am, what happened to you on August 4th, 2000 at approximately 4 o'clock in the morning?
(Señora, qué le sucedió a usted el 4 de agosto del 2000, aproximadamente a las 4 de la mañana)
IF:¿Qué fue lo que le sucedió a usted el día 4 de agosto del 2000 aproximadamente a las 4 de la mañana?

In example 1, the level of formality in the original utterance is not preserved in the female interpreter's rendition. The effect on the witness may be negative because the witness may perceive, incorrectly, that the attorney's question is face threatening and disrespectful.

These results, at first glance, could be interpreted as being somewhat unexpected. Female interpreters in the study are aware of the formality of the courtroom and females have often been perceived as being more deferential than men and more in tune with the need not to impose or offend. The question, hence, that arises, is, why the differences? The answer may lie in the way female interpreters manage memory load, which may be mediated by women's socialization. To test this theory, I segment the data by various turn lengths and by gender. The purpose of this segmentation is to examine whether the differences in gender that are observed, on average, for all turn lengths are also observed with utterances that are six or fewer words, nine or fewer words, and ten or more words.

With utterances that are six or fewer words and nine or fewer words, I find that the relationship between gender and the omission of forms of address is not statistically significant for either male (IM) or female interpreters (IF):

(2) A: When were you hired, *sir*?
(¿Cuándo lo contrataron a usted, señor)?
IF: ¿Cuándo lo contrataron, *señor*?

(3) A: Do you work in Connecticut, *sir*?
(¿Trabaja usted en Connecticut, señor?)
IM: ¿Trabaja en Connecticut, *señor*?

At ten words or more, the differences between the genders and the omission of the linguistic variable *terms of address* began to rise and are significant:

(4) A: At the time of the accident, if there was no padlock in the door of a switching unit like this one, it would be your office that would be in

charge of going there and placing the padlock, right *Mr. J*?

(Al momento del accidente si no hubiese un candado en la puerta de un transformador como este, sería la responsabilidad de su oficina de ir allí y poner un candado, ¿no es cierto *Señor J*?)

IF: Al momento del accidente si no hay un candado en la puerta de un transformador como este, sería la responsabilidad de la oficina de usted de asegurarse y poner un candado, ¿cierto?

(5) A: I'm showing you here what's been marked as plaintiff's exhibit number one. It shows the names and positions for the 2002 fiscal year. They are listed on the table. Do you recognize the names of any of the persons listed *Mrs. M*?

(Le muestro lo que ha sido marcado como prueba instrumental uno de la parte demandante. Incluye los nombres y los cargos para el año fiscal 2002. Estan listados en la tabla. ¿Reconoce usted alguno de los nombres de las personas en la lista, señora *M*?

IM: Le muestro lo que ha sido marcado exhibit uno de la parte demandante. Demuestra los nombres y los puestos para el año fiscal 2002 que están incluidos en la tabla. ¿Reconoce usted los nombres de alguna de las personas en la lista, *Sra. M*?

The effect of the female interpreter's omission can be best appreciated by describing the attorney's strategy. In example 4, the attorney's use of *Señor J* (Mr. J) seems to soften the face threatening nature of the attorney's question. The attorney is, basically, implying that the negligence of the witness's employer and, indirectly, the witness himself, were responsible for the plaintiff's injuries. The attorney wants to make his point across, but does not want to alienate the witness or seem too harsh in the eyes of the jurors. His use of a deference marker such as "Mr. J" may assist the attorney in achieving that objective. The attorney's strategy, however, is conveyed in a lengthy and somewhat dense utterance.

Although the length of the utterance does not have a significant effect on the male interpreter's rendition of a comparable question that includes an utterance final term of address such as *Señora M* (Mrs. M) (example 5), it has a significant effect on the female interpreter's rendition of a term of address (example 4). The female interpreter maintains, for the most part, the syntactic and lexical qualities of the original, but she sacrifices the linguistic elements that designate social moves.

The possible explanations for the female interpreter's treatment of deference may stem from a cognitive and sociolinguistic source. Hence, I will use a combined approach, which accounts for both cognitive and sociolinguistic factors. It is important to note, that the explanations here are only suggestive, given the small sample of female and male interpreters that comprise the data.

Socialization seems to play a role in the manner in which men and women store and retrieve information. As Colley (2002:577) and her colleagues propose, "differences between men's and women's gender role socialization may result in variations in the amount of internal representations that guide information seeking and retrieval, and hence influence memory for gender-related information." Women, for example, may be better at recalling events that are person-oriented or that focus on what linguists such as Tannen (1990) have described as "promoting intimacy and solidarity." Address forms, such as "Sir" and "Mr/Mrs," are key indicators of how speakers position their addressees and, hence, may not further the building of horizontal ties (Eckert and McConnell-Ginet 2003). In the context of the courtroom, attorneys are aware that not coming across as respectful may breed hostility with both the witness and the jurors. Female interpreters are also aware of the attorney's use of strategy and are able to capture the attorney's tone in short utterances when their processing capacity is not taxed. Once the length of a turn increases, however, female interpreters make a linguistic and possibly cognitive-based choice to omit those variables that indicate deference and diminish solidarity.

The notion that women are socialized to reject hierarchies and promote intimacy and solidarity, particularly when addressing women, may explain the female interpreters' failure to encode these terms of address efficiently. They are able to recall them only when memory load is low and awareness of their role in the courtroom is high. In this sense, an increase in memory load interferes with the female interpreter's ability to maintain her prescribed role in the courtroom and place sufficient listening effort on those linguistic features that she may have been socialized not to value as much. The interpreter's rendition, thus, shows a focus on the syntactic and lexical features of the original, which she may consciously or unconsciously deem more relevant.

The notion that socialization plays a role in the interpreter's processing and reconstruction of language needs to be researched further. The data set is small and studies on women's speech have traditionally examined the linguistic aspects of female-to-female interaction. More analysis is needed to account for the omissions of terms of address when both men and women are also addressed. In this study, a preliminary analysis of the data indicates that female interpreters had a higher error rate of omissions of terms of address when attorneys were addressing a female witness (0.250743) than when they were addressing a male witness (0.043079). They omitted significantly with both genders. These results are insightful, and with a larger data set, it may be found that these error rates are significantly correlated only with female witnesses. This finding would further the notion that a need for solidarity and intimacy is triggered when the female interpreter's processing capacity is taxed and recall is affected by socialization-based factors.

In addition to socialization, cultural factors (Lakoff & Ide 2005; Mitchell-Kernan 1972) may explain some of the differences observed in the data. These factors should be examined to establish whether the socialization of female interpreters of a specific socio cultural background accounts for the female interpreters not changing their strategy, regardless of the gender of the witness. This is of particular interest because the use of terms of address is a prominent and common feature of Spanish-speaking Latin America and would have been expected in the female interpreters' renditions. The influence of English, which on average may be less formal and hierarchical, should be investigated also.

Female Interpreters' Treatment of Politeness

Polite terms such as "please" conventionally signal to an addressee that the speaker's request may carry some type of imposition. Because the speaker cares about the possible harm to the addressee's negative face (Brown and Levinson 1987; Goffman 1967), he or she mitigates the potential imposition by using politeness formulas. Negative face, for example, is defined as a speaker's need not to be interfered with and to be recognized and respected as an individual. Attorneys can use negative politeness strategically to reduce the degree of imposition that their questions may have on their addressees. At short turn lengths, female interpreters maintain the tone of the attorney's original questions and, as expected, do not add to, or omit from, the attorney's exchanges politeness markers:

(6) A: *Please* tell us what happened there?
    IF: *¿Por favor* díganos que pasó allí?

At turn lengths of ten words or higher, female interpreters start to add politeness markers, which affects the attorney's strategy:

(7) A: In the table you have in front of you, there is a list of names and positions. Tell the members of the jury if you know any of the individuals listed on that table.
    (En la tabla que tiene frente a usted hay una lista de nombres y puestos. Dígale a los miembros del jurado si usted conoce a alguno de los individuos en la tabla)
    IF: En la tabla que tiene al frente suyo hay una lista de nombres y puestos. *Por favor*, dígale a los miembros del jurado si usted conoce a alguno de los individuos incluidos en la tabla.

Here the attorney's strategy is virtually a command. It is not structured as an indirect request, such as "could you tell the members of the jury," nor does it include a politeness marker such as "please." The attorney, who is cross-examining the witness, does not wish to recognize that the witness's negative face may have been threatened by having to reveal her relationship with her former co-worker, who, like her, was a political appointee, but who, unlike her, was not fired with the change in government. During the cross-examination of this witness, the attorney often showed her feelings of antipathy toward the witness by insinuating that the witness was not being truthful or upfront with her claims. The attorney's displeasure with the witness is clearly evident in her cross-examination style.

The female interpreter, however, did not follow the attorney's lead at higher-turn lengths. The explanation for the interpreter's addition of "please" may be consonant with that for the omission of terms of address. An increase in memory load may have prompted the female interpreter, either consciously or unconsciously, to add information in an attempt to compensate for possible loss of recall during the listening or comprehension phase. The choice of linguistic content added is possibly due to gender-specific factors, which serve to promote solidarity with the witness and minimize imposition. In this sense increasing turn length acts as a trigger, but the interpreter's socialization determines the nature of the interpreter's addition in a particular context. In this case, the addition serves to promote the witness's negative face, which seems to be a bigger concern for female than for male interpreters.

I must note that I considered the possibility that type of examination (i.e., direct or cross-examination) and the gender of the witness may have affected the rate of errors for these types of additions. Hence, I segmented the data for type of examination, gender, and turn length. The results suggest that the female interpreters' rate of addition of politeness markers is not significantly related to the witness or attorney's gender. That is, the interpreter added face-saving content with both male and female witnesses, as turn length rises. The addition of politeness markers, however, is correlated with examination style. Additions of politeness markers are observed at a significant rate ($t = 4.31256$) with the attorneys' cross-examination of witnesses. This is insightful because it provides further support for the possible relationship between socialization and encoding of linguistic content.

The data that includes cross-examinations are often lengthy and contentious. Thus, what could be derived from this relationship is that cognitive overload may be the trigger for gender-specific interpreting errors. The face-threatening nature of the examination accounts for the manner in which female interpreters encode politeness markers and perform their renditions.

THE MALE INTERPRETER'S PERSPECTIVE

Socialization appears to have also influenced male interpreters' treatment of disagreement and politeness in the data at increasing turn lengths. Male

Table 6.3. The Relationship between Gender and Rate of Errors: The Discourse Marker "Well" and Politeness Markers

	Discourse Marker "Well"		
	Parameters	Male	Female
Estimated Parameters			
Estimated Coefficient		0.31356	0.02379
T-Statistic		(3.26371)	(1.60013)
Adjusted R-squared	0.18654		
	Politeness Markers		
	Parameters	Male	Female
Estimated Parameters			
Estimated Coefficient		0.21978	0.12891
T-Statistic		(2.84228)	(0.04918)
Adjusted R-squared	0.26801		

interpreters, for example, omit the discourse marker "well" and politeness markers such as "please" at a significant rate, as it is illustrated in Table 6.3. The differences in error rates and the difference in *t*-statistic for male and female interpreters suggest that male interpreters react to increasing turn length by omitting content that signals disagreement in a witness's response, such as the marker "well," and that function to save an addressee's negative face, such as "please." Both of these gender-specific errors appear to be influenced by male's focus on hierarchy and status and are discussed in detail in the following sections.

Male Interpreters' Treatment of the Discourse Marker "Well"

In the bilingual courtroom, pragmatic markers such as "well" are used often by witnesses to preface disagreements, such as, of the "yes, but" type (Pomerantz 1975). These types of markers are often observed in the attorneys' cross-examination of witnesses. They are rarely added to or omitted from either the male or female interpreters' renditions with turn lengths of six or fewer words or nine or fewer words:

(8) A: Did you get out of the car when the police officer asked?
   IM: ¿Se bajó del coche cuando el policía se lo pidió?
   W: *Bueno*, yo traté pero tenía miedo.
   IM: *Well*, I tried but I was afraid.

(9) A: Who went to the party?
     IF: ¿Quiénes fueron a la fiesta?
     W: Bueno, pienso que mi primo y yo solamente.
     IF: *Well*, I think only my cousin and myself.

As with other examples in this chapter that examine shorter turn lengths, the interpreters, regardless of their gender, are able to maintain all of the essential pragmatic content of the original. At ten or more words, however, the omission of this linguistic variable in the male interpreters' renditions starts to rise:

(10) A: Okay. Let's start with Ms. V. M. How do you know her, if for any reason?
      IM: Comencemos con la Sra. V. M. ¿Por qué la conoce usted, si por alguna razón?
      W: *Bueno*, ella en los años que yo trabajé en la oficina de reciclaje ella trabajaba para la oficina de personal. Fue mi compañera de trabajo, aunque no trabajábamos en la misma oficina.
      (Well, she, in the years that I worked at the recycling office, worked at the human resources office. She was my co-worker, although we did not work in the same office.)
      IM: In the years that I worked at the recycling office, she worked at the personnel office, and she was my co-worker. We didn't work in the same office.

In example 10, the attorney's strategy during this part of his cross-examination is to establish how well the plaintiff knew the person who allegedly terminated her position. The attorney, in an attempt to avoid an objection from opposing counsel on the grounds of the question being leading, ended his question with the clause "if for any reason." The witness responds by showing disagreement with what is implied in the attorney's question. She prefaces her response with the discourse marker "well," which signals her need to establish that she knew V. M., but in the capacity of co-worker. The male interpreter's rendition does not include the witness's marker and thus fails to capture the witness's need to demonstrate how and why she knows the defendant.

It is difficult to say precisely why the male interpreters omit the discourse marker "well" at higher turn lengths. One possible explanation, among others, is that the omission of this discourse marker is consistent with the male interpreters' apparent appreciation for the formality of the courtroom and its hierarchical nature. The witnesses' use of "well" often carries a confrontational tone, which seems to signal disagreement or lack of appreciation for the attorney's style of questioning. If the male interpreters perceive the attorneys to be in a position of power over the witnesses and they value that authority, then it is plausible that as their memory is increasingly taxed, they will no longer maintain those linguistic features that they deem unnecessary for a particular exchange or that do not respect the hierarchical structure of the courtroom.

Another possible, and complementary, explanation is that male interpreters are less able to recall some discourse markers that occur almost exclusively at utterance-initial position, such as "well." This is an intriguing proposition, because it suggests that there may be significant differences between the manner in which male and female interpreters store and recall discourse markers that appear predominantly or exclusively at onset-initial position. Furthermore, it provides additional evidence of the role that the position of a linguistic variable may play in its accurate rendition. In this study, however, in most of the instances in which male interpreters must render the discourse marker "well," it appears at onset-initial position. Hence, there is not sufficient data to test also the interpreters' treatment of utterance-final "well." Further study is necessary to establish whether the location of this discourse marker, coupled with the length of the utterance, helps explain the male interpreters' lack of recall of the marker "well."

MALE INTERPRETER'S OMISSION
OF POLITENESS MARKERS

Male interpreters in this study remarked that counsel's ability to strategize and maintain control over the witnesses needed to be conveyed clearly in their renditions. They were able to maintain the attorneys' use of politeness strategies at shorter turn lengths. The attorneys' strategy, however, suffered at higher turn lengths because male interpreters consistently omitted this type of marker:

(11) A: Those facts at that time when you gave this sworn statement were clear in your mind; where they not?
       IM: ¿No es cierto que cuando usted dio esta declaración jurada los acontecimientos que habían occurido esa noche los tenía frescos en su mente?
       W: Eso es correcto.
       IM: That's correct.
       A: So when the police hit José he had already been fighting the police officers. He was resisting arrest. Fighting the police. Could you *please* tell us if that is what what you said in your sworn statement?
       (Así que cuando la policía le dío a José ya había estado en un forsejeo con los policías. Estaba resistiendo el arresto. Peleando con la policía.

¿Podría decirnos, por favor, si eso es lo que usted dijo en su declaración jurada?)

IM: De manera que cuando la policía le dio a José, ya José había estado en un forcejeo con la policía. Estaba resistiendo el arresto. Peleando. ¿Es eso lo que usted indíca en su declaración jurada?

The male interpreter's omission of a politeness marker, such as "please," alters the attorney's intent to save the witness's face. To understand the extent of the effect of the male interpreter's rendition on counsel's strategy, it is important to provide some background information about the case. The plaintiff in this case alleges that he was the victim of police brutality. The plaintiff, while attending a party with some friends and his brother, was arrested for violating the terms of a restraining order. The plaintiff's former girlfriend, who had requested the restraining order, was also at the party when the plaintiff arrived. The police were called, and when they arrived at the premises, they attempted to arrest the plaintiff, whom they claim was intoxicated, belligerent, and resisting arrest. During the course of the trial, many witnesses for both the plaintiff and the defense provided their testimony. In example 11, the attorney for the defense is cross-examining the plaintiff's brother, who was an eyewitness to the alleged beating of the plaintiff by the police. The witness had been very emotional during direct examination and had cried at different points of his testimony when recounting the police's alleged assault. During the defense attorney's cross-examination, the attorney asked the witness whether the police had hit the plaintiff after the plaintiff had been allegedly resisting arrest. The intent of the attorney's question is possibly to establish that the plaintiff had initiated the aggression and that the police were responding in just fashion. The attorney, however, wished to do so without challenging the witness's face unnecessarily. The witness had shown vulnerability throughout his testimony, and it is possibly in the best interest of the defense attorney to be cautious in his handling of this witness. The attorney's intent, however, is not fully captured in the male interpreter's rendition.

Although the effect of the interpreter's rendition on the attorney's strategy can be derived clearly from the example, it does not reveal why the interpreter omits the use of a politeness marker, such as "please." The explanations for the male interpreter's manipulation of politeness markers, as was the case with the female interpreters, may lie, in part, in his response to increasing turn length and to socialization factors.

Male interpreters, when faced with increased turn length, may not place much listening or cognitive effort to encoding linguistic information that is aimed at promoting goodwill and reducing negative face. Politeness markers, such as "please," signal recognition that the request imposes on the addressee and that the speaker cares about not threatening the addressees' negative face.

The function of "please," thus, is to mitigate the request, and it is central to the attorney's strategy. The use of this type of marker, however, particularly when the addressee is male, as is the case with this witness, takes away from the speaker's position of dominance. Male interpreters may place significant attention to the use of markers, such as "please," only when the attorney is addressing a woman or when the length of an utterance is low and the interpreters' ability to listen for and recall linguistic content is at its highest point.

To test this hypothesis and also the possibility that type of examination (i.e., direct or cross-examination), may affect the rate of errors for politeness markers omitted, I segmented the data for type of examination, gender, and turn length. The results suggest that the male interpreters' rate of omissions of politeness is significantly related to the witnesses' gender (male), but is not significantly related to the attorneys' gender or to the use of direct vs. cross-examination. What could be derived from these findings is that men omit politeness most often when their processing capacity is taxed and when the witness is male. The male interpreter may place more listening effort on politeness markers when the witness is female, possibly because men have been socialized to assume that women expect or require more politeness (Holmes 1995). The male interpreter does not extend this treatment to males as the length of an utterance increases. In this sense, the male interpreters' recall may be affected if they construct male witnesses to be less vulnerable than female witnesses and place less listening effort on those linguistic variables that designate politeness.

There are various possible explanations for the linguistic behavior observed in this chapter. I have focused mostly on explanations that are rooted in sociolinguistic research and that may be combined with studies that examine the relationship between socialization and cognition. To have a clearer understanding of the role that gender may play in the types of errors observed in the bilingual courtroom and the possible causes of gender-related errors, future studies that examine a larger data set and other cultural, linguistic, and cognitive factors are needed. The findings of this, and future research, may provide the legal interpreting community with a clearer picture of the role that gender may need to play in the training of courtroom interpreters.

THE TRAINING OF COURTROOM INTERPRETERS: CONSIDERING THE EFFECT OF GENDER ON THE EXAMINATION PROCESS

The results presented in this chapter indicate that male and female interpreters make different types of errors, specifically as the length of a turn increases.

Although these findings can suggest only that there may be significant differences between male and female interpreters, the implications of the findings to the law and to the study of memory recall in consecutive interpreting demand that the role of gender be considered further in the training of female and male interpreters.

First, the court-interpreting profession and those who provide them with training should be made aware of the possible impact that gender-specific-induced errors may have on the outcome of a trial. This is of particular importance, because the majority of court interpreters are female. My findings, for example, suggest that female interpreters omit, at a higher rate than male interpreters, those linguistic markers that indicate deference, and, add those that indicate politeness. The omission of deference, for example, may have significant consequences for both attorneys and witnesses. Interpreters who omit deference markers from the attorneys' questions may change the tone of the attorneys' examination strategy. The witness may perceive, incorrectly, that the attorney has little or no respect for his or her person, which may prompt the witness to be less forward and courteous with his or her responses. The attorney's apparent lack of respect and the witness's response may in turn trigger a negative perception from jurors, particularly those of Hispanic origin (Berk-Seligson 2002).

The tone of a witness's response may also determine the style of the attorney's subsequent questions. In this sense, counsel's strategy is not only affected in that instance in which the female interpreter omitted a term of address, but it is potentially affected for a significant portion of counsel's subsequent examination of the witness.

The male interpreter's omissions may also have a detrimental effect on both counsel's strategy and on jurors' perception of a witness. On the one hand, the interpreter's omission of the witness's use of the discourse marker "well" may result in a more convincing and powerful response. On the other hand, the attorney's omission of politeness markers may signal to the witness that the attorney does not respect him or her. This impression could shift the attorney's strategy from one that is cordial and respectful to one that is hostile and unmitigating.

Second, the training of court interpreters may need to account for the possible differences between the genders and their response to increased memory load. In Chapter 5, I discuss the potential uses of note taking in the bilingual courtroom. In light of my initial findings on gender, court interpreters could be trained to take notes that address specifically their differences. Female interpreters, for example, would be encouraged to be especially aware of their treatment of deference markers, such as "sir," and take notes that indicate the type of deference marker and its location in the utterance. Male interpreters, on the other hand, could be made aware of their consistent omission of markers that soften the imposition of a speech act, such as attorneys' use of politeness markers when making a request, and of pragmatic markers that indicate disagreement with an attorney's line of questioning, such as the marker "well." Male interpreters, like their female counterparts, may be trained to focus on those linguistic features that they omit most often and to account for them in their notes. In this sense, court interpreters could be trained to place more listening effort on those linguistic features that they seem not to recall consistently because of their gender.

SUMMARY

The differences in error rates for male and female interpreters suggest that the gender of the interpreter may play a role in how specific linguistic variables are treated as turn length increases. Female interpreters seem to be more prone to omit those linguistic features that signal deference. As turn length increases, female interpreters also add politeness markers that are not present in the original. Male interpreters, on the other hand, seem to omit politeness markers, such as "please," and the discourse marker "well" at a significant rate.

The explanations for the types of errors observed in the male and female interpreters' renditions are varied and may include cognitive, sociolinguistic, and cultural variations. The notion that women are socialized to reject hierarchies and promote intimacy and solidarity, for example, may explain the female interpreters' failure to listen for and encode terms of address efficiently. Female interpreters seem to be able to recall terms of address only when memory load is low and when awareness for the context of the courtroom and their role in the courtroom is high. In this sense, an increase in memory load seems to have interfered with the female interpreters' ability to maintain their prescribed role in the courtroom. Cognitive overload may have prompted them to focus on what they perceive to be the most important linguistic features of an utterance. The interpreters' renditions show a focus on the syntactic and lexical features of the original, which they may consciously or unconsciously deem more relevant.

When turn length rises, female interpreters may also react by adding politeness markers to the original. These markers may serve to signal solidarity and empathy, which are feelings the female interpreter may be socialized to particularly use in a context such as the courtroom. This addition, however, affects counsel's strategy. Counsel, for example, may have preferred to impose on the witness rather than to minimize imposition, as it is reflected in the female interpreter's rendition.

Male interpreters differ from female interpreters in that they omit the discourse marker "well" and politeness markers, such as "please." The possible explanations for the male interpreters behavior may reflect the need to reconcile their responsibilities in the courtroom with their response to memory load. The male interpreters' omission of the discourse marker "well" at higher turn lengths may be due to various causes. One possible explanation, among others, is that the omission of this discourse marker is consistent with the male interpreters' apparent appreciation for the formality of the courtroom and its hierarchical nature. The witnesses' use of "well" often carried a confrontational tone, which seems to signal disagreement or lack of appreciation for the attorneys' style of questioning. If the male interpreters perceive the attorneys to be in a position of power, then it is plausible that as their memory is increasingly taxed they will not place much listening and/or memory effort on those linguistic features that they deem unnecessary for a particular exchange or that do not respect the hierarchical structure of the courtroom. It is also plausible that male interpreters are less able to recall some discourse markers that occur almost exclusively at onset-initial position, such as "well." This is an intriguing proposition, because it suggests that there may be significant differences between the manner in which male and female interpreters store and recall discourse markers that appear predominantly or exclusively at utterance-initial position. This possibility needs to be studied further.

The male interpreters' omission of politeness markers may also signal a lack of focus on those linguistic features that reduce imposition on the addressee. At higher turn lengths, when texts are voluminous, the male interpreter's socialization may have an effect on recall and may significantly affect how he renders some of the linguistic variables in the data, particularly politeness markers.

In sum, there are many possible explanations for the linguistic differences among the genders discussed in this chapter. The impact of memory load, however, appears to be significant and is, at the very least, a trigger for the differences observed between the male and female interpreters' rendition of some linguistic content. To have a clearer understanding of the role that gender may play in the types of errors observed in the bilingual courtroom, future studies that examine a larger data set and other cultural, linguistic, and cognitive factors are needed. The findings of these studies may have direct implications on the future training of courtroom interpreters and on the way that gender is addressed in the bilingual courtroom.

NOTE

1. In this estimation, the variable *gender* was treated as a dummy variable. Dummy variables are binary, taking the value of either zero or one. In the case of gender, one is used to denote female interpreters, and zero is used to denote male interpreters.

Chapter Seven

Conclusions

THE IMPLICATIONS OF THE FINDINGS: A SUMMARY

At the beginning of this study, I discussed the relationship between an individual's constitutional right to due process and an individual's right to an interpreter. The groundbreaking case of U.S. ex rel Negrón v. N.Y., for example, demonstrates that without the presence of an interpreter, a non-English-speaking defendant is deprived of the most basic right of being "present" at his or her own trial. The outcome of Negrón's case, coupled with the outcry of linguistic minorities for equal protection under the law, led the way to the enactment of the Court Interpreters Act of 1978. This Act, which guarantees the right to a court-appointed interpreter to witnesses and defendants who speak only or primarily a language other than English, was instrumental in the professionalization of the interpreting profession.

After the passing of the Court Interpreters Act of 1978, certification became the standard for courtroom interpreters who worked in the federal courts. The establishment of professional organizations, such as NAJIT, also played an important role in establishing a code of ethics and responsibilities for courtroom interpreters to follow when carrying out their duties in the courtroom. The interpreters' responsibilities, according to NAJIT, include providing a faithful rendition of the original message without any distortions, additions, omissions, explanations, or paraphrasing.

The rationale behind insisting that courtroom interpreters convey all of the linguistic elements of the original, although important for the professionalization of the legal interpreting profession, was found to be an unfulfilled expectation. Ethnolinguistic studies such as Berk-Seligson's (2002) and Hale's (2004) reveal that interpreters consistently add, omit, and change the original message. These studies also demonstrate that there are repercussions to the interpreters changing the linguistic content and style of the original, because jurors' perception of witnesses may be affected by language use in the courtroom.

The significance of the findings of prior research prompted me to investigate the possible cognitive reasons for some of the interpreters' treatment of key linguistic variables. The main findings of this research point to the significant relationship between utterance length and the interpreters' treatment of style, syntax, meaning, and intent. The results of the analysis show that turn length explains about 38 percent of the total errors observed in the data. Although I expected turn length to affect the interpreters' processing capacity, the extent of the effect on the quality of the interpreters' rendition of key linguistic variables had not been quantified prior to this study.

The findings of this study also suggest that the error rates for the linguistic variables studied increased with the segmentation of the data. The results show that the error rate for total omissions increased at an increasing, rather than a constant, rate. What this means is that increasing turn length causes interpreters to make more omissions than additions. These findings have both linguistic and cognitive implications. They suggest that the effect of turn length on memory may result in the interpreter altering the register and style of the original, often times from a *powerless* style to a *powerful* one. In light of prior studies, the effects of cognitive overload on the interpreting process and the possible outcome of a trial seem to be significant.

The empirical findings suggest that researchers and practitioners of courtroom interpreting may need to direct their efforts more aggressively to finding strategies that assist in reducing cognitive overload. I addressed the costs and possible benefits of two strategies that interpreters in this study used to reduce the effects of turn length on their processing abilities: interruptions and semiconsecutive interpreting.

Interpreters chose most often to interrupt the witnesses. This seems to be one of the preferred modes of managing textual density and volume in the courtroom. The two most common points in a turn of talk that interpreters chose to interrupt were either at an inappropriate grammatical juncture or after the witness had provided a great deal of information. The former may lead to errors because the interpreter chooses to interrupt when he or she expects more information from the speaker than he or she can handle rather than at a point in discourse that provides sufficient grammatical content. The latter led to errors, because the interpreter waited too long to interrupt. The average length at which the interpreters in this study interrupt is 22 words. This results in about 0.3 errors per interrupted event.

For interruptions, the rate of errors was not statistically significant with total additions. The results for total omissions, however, were significant and consistent with those findings on the effect of turn length reported in Chapter 3. The results indicate that interpreters make 0.86 omissions per every interrupted turn of talk. This means that for every 100 interruptions, interpreters will make 86 omissions. These omissions are the cost of the interpreters using interruptions as a means to reduce memory load. When these results are examined, next to those for the entire data, they strongly suggest that lack of recall is the most affected cognitive factor in courtroom interpreting. From a pragmatics perspective, this may translate to the witnesses' original utterances being rendered in a powerful style more often than a powerless style. In the case of pragmatic markers, such as hesitations and the marker "well," this may lead to a more favorable outcome for the witness.

Semiconsecutive interpreting, on the other hand, affected the source language discourse the least. This mode of interpreting reduced turn length by 1.3 words to an average length of 8.9 words. When these results are compared with those of interrupting the witness, the improved reduction in turn length is evident (10.25). The difference between the average length of a turn that uses semiconsecutive interpreting, and the average length of a turn in which the interpreter relies on interrupting (21.75), is approximately 11 words. Because shorter segment lengths are associated with fewer errors, the results for semiconsecutive interpreting show a reduction in errors in the courtroom, specifically in omissions. This mode of interpreting seems to address the issue of cognitive overload best and thus produced lower error rates than interruptions.

In light of the findings with interruptions and semiconsecutive interpreting, court interpreters should rethink their use of interruptions to manage cognitive overload. This strategy seems to carry more costs than actual benefits. The use of semiconsecutive interpreting, though, seems to carry a net benefit, may also have limitations, albeit of a different kind, that need to be considered further.

The practicality of using semiconsecutive interpreting as a strategy to manage cognitive overload in the courtroom may be questioned. Semiconsecutive interpreting depends on others for its execution. The interpreters, though they may benefit from the technique, do not have direct control of the use of semiconsecutive interpreting. Thus, interpreters must depend on others who may not be inclined to self-segmenting their output. The result is a strategy that has its merits, but that may not be easily implemented in the courtroom. The most significant finding of this study may lie in what the results suggest. The results clearly point to the need to use techniques in the courtroom that the interpreter can control, and that properly manage memory load, such as note taking.

Although note taking seems to be commonly used in other venues that use consecutive interpreting, such as conference interpreting, court interpreters have not fully embraced the use of notes when providing renditions in the courtroom. I propose that the court interpreting community should examine more closely the possible benefits of note taking, given its potential uses as a memory reinforcer.

The findings presented in Chapters 3 and 4 point to a significant relationship between increasing turn length and the linguistic variables that seem to affect the most the pragmatic and semantic properties of the original, particularly those that may sway jurors' opinions of witnesses and attorneys. Interpreting, even in the best of the scenarios, takes up a great deal of mental effort. As turn length increases, the interpreter's performance seems to deteriorate significantly. Note taking, if performed correctly, may act as an effective memory reinforcer and assist the interpreter in having better recall of the original.

The choice of language and code seems to be key to the satisfactory use of note taking in consecutive interpreting. The preliminary findings of prior research seem to suggest that taking notes in the source or native language is better than in the target or foreign language. In the context of the courtroom, these preliminary findings could be used to encourage interpreters to take notes in the source or native language. Court interpreters should be encouraged also to take economical notes—that is, not verbatim notes and in a code that is easy to recall. The notes may need to include those linguistic components that often seem to be forgotten in this mode of interpreting, such as pragmatic and extralinguistic markers. This, however, may not be necessary if it is found that note taking improves the recall of all linguistic content.

The future of note taking as an effective strategy to reduce errors in the bilingual courtroom, however, depends on the findings of future research. An informal exercise on note taking with certified courtroom interpreters seems to point to the potential benefits of note taking, particularly with regard to the improved recall of pragmatic and stylistic markers. Researchers who specialize in the field and those who train courtroom interpreters, however, need to conduct controlled studies that provide significant empirical evidence on the potential benefits or costs of note taking. In Chapter 5, I lay out a methodological foundation for some of this research. The results of these studies, particularly if they prove that note taking is beneficial in the courtroom, may prompt the legal interpreting community to embrace the teaching of note taking and to apply it consistently in the courtroom.

The last issue addressed in this study was whether there are differences between the errors male and female interpreters make. I observed in my limited sample of interpreters that both genders made either the same type of errors or, less often, made different types of errors. The differences in error rates for male and female interpreters suggest that the gender of the interpreter may play a role in how specific linguistic variables are treated as turn length increases. Female interpreters, for example, seem to be more prone to omit those linguistic features that signal deference. As turn length increases, female interpreters also add politeness markers that further solidarity. Male interpreters, on the other hand, omitted the discourse marker "well" and politeness markers, such as "please," at a significant rate.

The explanations for the types of errors observed in the male and female interpreters' renditions are varied and may include cognitive, sociolinguistic, and cultural factors. The notion that women are socialized to reject hierarchies and promote intimacy and solidarity, for example, may explain the female interpreters' failure to encode terms of address efficiently. Female interpreters seem to be able to recall terms of address only when memory load is low and awareness for the context of the courtroom and their role in the courtroom is high. In this sense, an increase in memory load interferes with the female interpreters' ability to maintain their prescribed role in the courtroom and prompts them to omit what they perceive to be the least important linguistic features in a turn of talk. In these cases, the female interpreters' renditions show a focus on the syntactic and lexical features of the original, which they may consciously or unconsciously deem more relevant.

Male interpreters' treatment of discourse markers, such as "well" and politeness, as turn length rises may signal the need to reconcile their responsibilities in the courtroom with their response to memory load. The male interpreters' omissions at higher turn lengths may be due to various causes. One possible explanation, among others, is that the omission of the discourse marker "well" and politeness is consistent with the male interpreters' apparent appreciation of the formality of the courtroom and its hierarchical nature. If the male interpreters perceived the attorneys to be in a position of power and they value that authority, then it is plausible that as their memory is increasingly taxed, they will no longer maintain those linguistic features that they deem unnecessary for a particular exchange, or that do not respect the hierarchical structure of the courtroom. It is also plausible that the position of the linguistic variable, particularly of the marker "well," played a role in the male interpreters' recall of such a variable. This is an intriguing proposition, because it suggests that there may be significant differences between the manner that male and female interpreters store and recall discourse markers that appear predominantly, or exclusively, at utterance-initial position.

In sum, there may be various possible explanations for the linguistic behavior observed in this work. It is clear, however, that the impact of memory load is a significant factor in interpreter-induced errors. To have a clearer understanding of the role that memory load has on recall and on gender, future studies that examine a more varied data set are needed. The findings of these studies may have direct implications on the future training of courtroom interpreters and need to be pursued further. The errors that court interpreters make have significant implications for the attorneys, who need to be able to maintain control over their examination strategy, for the witnesses who need and have the right to get their testimony across accurately, and for the defendant who has the right to a fair trial.

Appendix One

Court Interpreters Act of 1978

United States Code, Title 28 §1827
(a)   The Director of the Administrative Office of the United States Courts shall establish a program to facilitate the use of certified and otherwise qualified interpreters in judicial proceedings instituted by the United States.
(b)

(1) The Director shall prescribe, determine, and certify the qualifications of persons who may serve as certified interpreters, when the Director considers certification of interpreters to be merited, for the hearing impaired (whether or not also speech impaired) and persons who speak only or primarily a language other than the English language, in judicial proceedings instituted by the United States. The Director may certify interpreters for any language if the Director determines that there is a need for certified interpreters in that language. Upon the request of the Judicial Conference of the United States for certified interpreters in a language, the Director shall certify interpreters in that language. Upon such a request from the judicial council of a circuit and the approval of the Judicial Conference, the Director shall certify interpreters for that circuit in the language requested. The judicial council of a circuit shall identify and evaluate the needs of the districts within a circuit. The Director shall certify interpreters based on the results of criterion-referenced performance examinations. The Director shall issue regulations to carry out this paragraph within 1 year after the date of the enactment of the Judicial Improvements and Access to Justice Act.

(2) Only in a case in which no certified interpreter is reasonably available as provided in subsection (d) of this section, including a case in which certification of interpreters is not provided under paragraph (1) in

a particular language, may the services of otherwise qualified interpreters be used. The Director shall provide guidelines to the courts for the selection of otherwise qualified interpreters, in order to ensure that the highest standards of accuracy are maintained in all judicial proceedings subject to the provisions of this chapter.

(3) The Director shall maintain a current master list of all certified interpreters and otherwise qualified interpreters and shall report periodically on the use and performance of both certified and otherwise qualified interpreters in judicial proceedings instituted by the United States and on the languages for which interpreters have been certified. The Director shall prescribe, subject to periodic review, a schedule of reasonable fees for services rendered by interpreters, certified or otherwise, used in proceedings instituted by the United States, and in doing so shall consider the prevailing rate of compensation for comparable service in other governmental entities.

(c)

(1) Each United States district court shall maintain on file in the office of the clerk, and each United States attorney shall maintain on file, a list of all persons who have been certified as interpreters by the Director in accordance with subsection (b) of this section. The clerk shall make the list of certified interpreters for judicial proceeding available upon request.

(2) The clerk of the court, or other court employee designated by the chief judge, shall be responsible for securing the services of certified interpreters and otherwise qualified interpreters required for proceedings initiated by the United States, except that the United States attorney is responsible for securing the services of such interpreters for governmental witnesses.

(d)

(1) The presiding judicial officer, with the assistance of the Director of the Administrative Office of the United States Courts, shall utilize the services of the most available certified interpreter, or when no certified interpreter is reasonably available, as determined by the presiding judicial officer, the services of an otherwise qualified interpreter, in judicial proceedings instituted by the United States, if the presiding judicial officer determines on such officer's own motion or on the motion of a party that such party (including a defendant in a criminal case), or a witness who may present testimony in such judicial proceedings—

(A) speaks only or primarily a language other than the English language; or

(B) suffers from a hearing impairment (whether or not suffering also from a speech impairment)

so as to inhibit such party's comprehension of the proceedings or communication with counsel or the presiding judicial officer, or so as to inhibit such witness' comprehension of questions and the presentation of such testimony.

(2) Upon the motion of a party, the presiding judicial officer shall determine whether to require the electronic sound recording of a judicial proceeding in which an interpreter is used under this section. In making this determination, the presiding judicial officer shall consider, among other things, the qualifications of the interpreter and prior experience in interpretation of court proceedings; whether the language to be interpreted is not one of the languages for which the Director has certified interpreters, and the complexity or length of the proceeding. In a grand jury proceeding, upon the motion of the accused, the presiding judicial officer shall require the electronic sound recording of the portion of the proceeding in which an interpreter is used.

(e)

(1) If any interpreter is unable to communicate effectively with the presiding judicial officer, the United States attorney, a party (including a defendant in a criminal case), or a witness, the presiding judicial officer shall dismiss such interpreter and obtain the services of another interpreter in accordance with this section.

(2) In any judicial proceedings instituted by the United States, if the presiding judicial officer does not appoint an interpreter under subsection (d) of this section, an individual requiring the services of an interpreter may seek assistance of the clerk of court or the Director of the Administrative Office of the United States Courts in obtaining the assistance of a certified interpreter.

(f)

(1) Any individual other than a witness who is entitled to interpretation under subsection (d) of this section may waive such interpretation in whole or in part. Such a waiver shall be effective only if approved by the presiding judicial officer and made expressly by such individual on the record after opportunity to consult with counsel and after the presiding judicial officer has explained to such individual, utilizing the services of the most available certified interpreter, or when no certified interpreter is reasonably available, as determined by the presiding judicial officer, the services of an otherwise competent interpreter, the nature and effect of the waiver.

(2) An individual who waives under paragraph (1) of this subsection the right to an interpreter may utilize the services of a noncertified interpreter of such individual's choice whose fees, expenses, and costs shall be paid

in the manner provided for the payment of such fees, expenses, and costs
of an interpreter appointed under subsection (d) of this section.

(g)

(1) There are authorized to be appropriated to the Federal judiciary, and
to be paid by the Director of the Administrative Office of the United
States Courts, such sums as may be necessary to establish a program to
facilitate the use of certified and otherwise qualified interpreters, and
otherwise fulfill the provisions of this section and the Judicial Improvements and Access to Justice Act, except as provided in paragraph (3).

(2) Implementation of the provisions of this section is contingent upon the
availability of appropriated funds to carry out the purposes of this section.

(3) Such salaries, fees, expenses, and costs that are incurred with respect
to Government witnesses (including for grand jury proceedings) shall,
unless direction is made under paragraph (4), be paid by the Attorney
General from sums appropriated to the Department of Justice.

(4) Upon the request of any person in any action for which interpreting
services established pursuant to subsection (d) are not otherwise provided, the clerk of the court, or other court employee designated by the
chief judge, upon the request of the presiding judicial officer, shall,
where possible, make such services available to that person on a cost-re-
imbursable basis, but the judicial officer may also require the prepay-
ment of the estimated expenses of providing such services.

(5) If the Director of the Administrative Office of the United States
Courts finds it necessary to develop and administer criterion-referenced
performance examinations for purposes of certification, or other examinations for the selection of otherwise qualified interpreters, the Director
may prescribe for each examination a uniform fee for applicants to take
such examination. In determining the rate of the fee for each examination, the Director shall consider the fees charged by other organizations
for examinations that are similar in scope or nature. Notwithstanding section 3302 (b) of title 31, the Director is authorized to provide in any con-
tract or agreement for the development or administration of examinations
and the collection of fees that the contractor may retain all or a portion
of the fees in payment for the services. Notwithstanding paragraph (6) of
this subsection, all fees collected after the effective date of this paragraph
and not retained by a contractor shall be deposited in the fund established
under section 1931 of this title and shall remain available until expended.

(6) Any moneys collected under this subsection may be used to reimburse
the appropriations obligated and disbursed in payment for such services.

(h) The presiding judicial officer shall approve the compensation and
expenses payable to interpreters, pursuant to the schedule of fees prescribed by the Director under subsection (b)(3).

(i) The term "presiding judicial officer" as used in this section refers to any judge of a United States district court, including a bankruptcy judge, a United States magistrate judge, and in the case of grand jury proceedings conducted under the auspices of the United States attorney, a United States attorney.

(j) The term "judicial proceedings instituted by the United States" as used in this section refers to all proceedings, whether criminal or civil, including pretrial and grand jury proceedings (as well as proceedings upon a petition for a writ of habeas corpus initiated in the name of the United States by a relator) conducted in, or pursuant to the lawful authority and jurisdiction of a United States district court. The term "United States district court" as used in this subsection includes any court which is created by an Act of Congress in a territory and is invested with any jurisdiction of a district court established by chapter 5 of this title.

(k) The interpretation provided by certified or otherwise qualified interpreters pursuant to this section shall be in the simultaneous mode for any party to a judicial proceeding instituted by the United States and in the consecutive mode for witnesses, except that the presiding judicial officer, sua sponte or on the motion of a party, may authorize a simultaneous, or consecutive interpretation when such officer determines after a hearing on the record that such interpretation will aid in the efficient administration of justice. The presiding judicial officer, on such officer's motion or on the motion of a party, may order that special interpretation services as authorized in section 1828 of this title be provided if such officer determines that the provision of such services will aid in the efficient administration of justice.

(l) Notwithstanding any other provision of this section or section 1828, the presiding judicial officer may appoint a certified or otherwise qualified sign language interpreter to provide services to a party, witness, or other participant in a judicial proceeding, whether or not the proceeding is instituted by the United States, if the presiding judicial officer determines, on such officer's own motion or on the motion of a party or other participant in the proceeding, that such individual suffers from a hearing impairment. The presiding judicial officer shall, subject to the availability of appropriated funds, approve the compensation and expenses payable to sign language interpreters appointed under this section in accordance with the schedule of fees prescribed by the Director under subsection (b)(3) of this section.

Appendix Two

Code of Ethics and Professional Responsibility (NAJIT)

PREAMBLE

Many persons who come before the courts are non- or limited-English speakers. The function of court interpreters and translators is to remove the language barrier to the extent possible, so that such persons' access to justice is the same as that of similarly situated English speakers for whom no such barrier exists. The degree of trust that is placed in court interpreters and the magnitude of their responsibility necessitate high, uniform ethical standards that will both guide and protect court interpreters in the course of their duties as well as uphold the standards of the profession as a whole.

While many ethical decisions are straightforward, no code of ethics can foresee every conceivable scenario; court interpreters cannot mechanically apply abstract ethical principles to every situation that may arise. This Code is therefore intended not only to set forth fundamental ethical precepts for court interpreters to follow, but also to encourage them to develop their own, well-informed ethical judgment.

APPLICABILITY

All NAJIT members are bound to comply with this Code.

CANON 1. ACCURACY

Source language speech should be faithfully rendered into the target language by conserving all the elements of the original message while accommodating the syntactic and semantic patterns of the target language. The rendition should sound natural in the target language, and there should be no distortion of the original message through addition or omission, explanation or paraphrasing. All hedges, false starts and repetitions should be conveyed; also, English words mixed into the other language should be retained, as should culturally bound terms which have no direct equivalent in English, or which may have more than one meaning. The register, style and tone of the source language should be conserved.

Guessing should be avoided. Court interpreters who do not hear or understand what a speaker has said should seek clarification. Interpreter errors should be corrected for the record as soon as possible.

CANON 2. IMPARTIALITY AND CONFLICTS OF INTEREST

Court interpreters and translators are to remain impartial and neutral in proceedings where they serve, and must maintain the appearance of impartiality and neutrality, avoiding unnecessary contact with the parties.

Court interpreters and translators shall abstain from comment on cases in which they serve. Any real or potential conflict of interest shall be immediately disclosed to the Court and all parties as soon as the interpreter or translator becomes aware of such conflict of interest.

CANON 3. CONFIDENTIALITY

Privileged or confidential information acquired in the course of interpreting or preparing a translation shall not be disclosed by the interpreter or translator without authorization.

CANON 4. LIMITATIONS OF PRACTICE

Court interpreters and translators shall limit their participation in those matters in which they serve to interpreting and translating, and shall avoid giving advice to the parties or otherwise engaging in activities that can be construed as the practice of law.

CANON 5. PROTOCOL AND DEMEANOR

Court interpreters shall conduct themselves in a manner consistent with the standards and protocol of the court, and shall perform their duties as unobtrusively as possible. Court interpreters are to use the same grammatical person as the speaker. When it becomes necessary to assume a primary role in the communication, they must make it clear that they are speaking for themselves.

CANON 6. MAINTENANCE AND IMPROVEMENT OF SKILLS AND KNOWLEDGE

Court interpreters and translators shall strive to maintain and improve their interpreting and translation skills and knowledge.

CANON 7. ACCURATE REPRESENTATION OF CREDENTIALS

Court interpreters and translators shall accurately represent their certifications, accreditations, training and pertinent experience.

CANON 8. IMPEDIMENTS TO COMPLIANCE

Court interpreters and translators shall bring to the Court's attention any circumstance or condition that impedes full compliance with any Canon of this Code, including interpreter fatigue, inability to hear, or inadequate knowledge of specialized terminology, and must decline assignments under conditions that make such compliance patently impossible.

Appendix Three

The Uses of the Regression Equation

In this study, a regression analysis is used to estimate the statistical relationship between the independent variables, such as turn length, and the dependent variables, such as additions. The best way to explain a regression is to provide a graphic representation.

A regression is a line fitted through observed data pairs (Bruning and Kintz, 1987; Kennedy, 1994). The data pairs record the number of, say, additions and turn length for each utterance. The regression line is fitted in such a way that for all turn lengths the lines minimize the sum of squared errors, which is also known as the sum of squared residuals. Regression errors measure the deviation of the observed actual pair from the regression line, as it is illustrated in Figure A.3.1. The estimated regression equation takes the following form: $y = \beta_1 C + \beta_2 x + e$. In this equation, y is the dependent variable and represents various forms of additions or omissions; C represents the regression constant; x represents the independent variable, such as turn length, and the dummy variables interruptions, semiconsecutive interpreting, and/or gender; β_1 and β_2 represent the estimated coefficients on the constant and turn length respectively; and e represents the regression residual. The estimated coefficient on turn length is the slope of the regression line, and the estimated coefficient on the constant term is the intercept term. A significant estimated coefficient suggests that the independent variable influences the regressant (such as the dependent variable total omissions). The relationship between the dependent variable (y) and the independent variable (x) is straightforward since the length of the witness' or attorney's original utterance (x) is not influenced by the interpreter's subsequent additions or omissions (y).

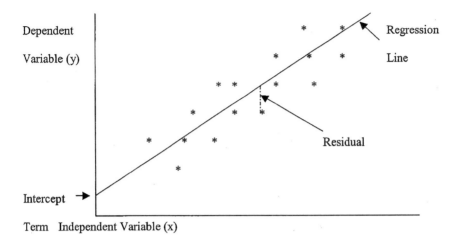

Figure A.3.1.   A Graphic Example of a Regression

To test whether the length of a witness or attorney's utterance causes the interpreter to add or omit information, each left-hand side variable is estimated individually against the constant and the length of a turn. In estimating the regressions, I examine whether turn length causes significant additions and omissions of any particular linguistic feature. I examine also the effect that increasing the length of a turn has on total additions and total omissions, and on the sum of total additions and total omissions, which I refer to as total events.

For each regression that I estimated, results were deemed to be significant if the t-statistic on the estimated coefficient was significant at a 95 percent confidence level. The t-statistic indicates whether the estimated coefficient on the regressor (the independent variable) is significant in a statistical sense. One other statistical measures of the goodness of fit will be reported also— adjusted R-squared.

The adjusted R-squared indicates the percentage of the variation of the regressant that is "explained" by the regression equation. For example, if the dependent variable is total omissions and the adjusted R-squared is 0.4, this indicates that 40 percent of the variation in total omissions is explained by turn length (the right-hand side regressor). An omitted regressor may explain the remaining 60 percent of the variation, which may be due to environmental or other cognitive factors, such as audio quality, stress/fatigue, and interpreter's level of competence, among others.

The data was also examined for the presence of non-linearity. Non-linearity may overestimate and underestimate the effect of the independent variable on the dependent variable. To account for the effects of non-linearity in the data, I tested for nonlinear relationships between the independent variables and the dependent variables. This test consisted of comparing regression results for groups of data below and above different turn lengths. It is important to note that in this part of the analysis I am not interested in examining the specific functional relationship between the independent and dependent variables, but rather in determining whether error rates change with longer turn lengths. If a nonlinear relationship exists it will manifest itself in statistically different estimated coefficients on the independent variable. Figure A.3.2 depicts the estimated relationship of nonlinear data.

In the above figure, the true relationship between the dependent variable (y) and the independent variable (x) is nonlinear (the curve). The regression fits a line to minimize the sum of squared residuals. The estimated value of the dependent variable is approximately 4 when the independent variable is 10. On average, the true relationship is for the independent variable to have a value less than 4 when the independent variable is 10, but rarely is the relationship perfect. More often than not, the observed value is equal to neither the true relationship nor the estimated relationship. Hence, there is a residual that accounts for the difference between the estimated value and the observed value.

In the case of nonlinear data, linear regressions may not describe well the true relationship between the dependent and the independent variable. I have chosen instead to divide the data into sub-samples and regress the dependent variable on each sub-sample of the independent variable. Figure A.3.3 depicts two regressions over the data originally presented in Figure A.3.2. In figure A.3.3, the slope for the regression on B is steeper than that on A. This reflects higher error rates as the independent variable increases.

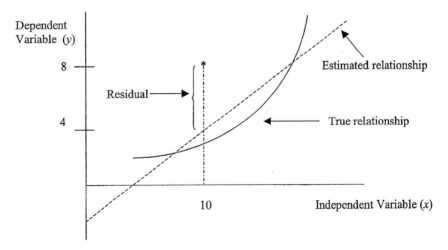

Figure A.3.2.   Depicting Non Linear Data in a Regression Line

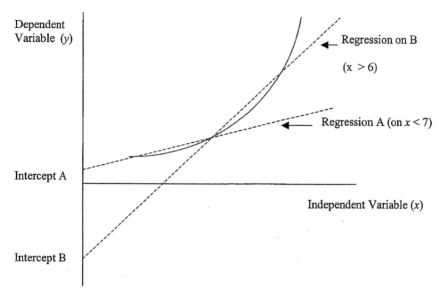

Figure A.3.3. Depicting Regressions on Segmented Data

Appendix 4

T-test Results by
Type of Interpreting Error

Type of error	Additions	Omissions	Changes
Dependent Variables			
Politeness Markers	—	2.94	—
Forms of Address	—	4.18	—
Active to Passive	—	—	2.81
Passive to Active	—	—	3.36
Focus Change	—	—	2.23
Verb Change	—	—	2.65
Lexical Change	—	—	2.87
Speech Disfluencies	2.85	3.76	—
Hedges "Well"	—	2.84	—
Discourse Markers	3.8	8.69	—
General Statements	—	2.19	—

Appendix 5

Text of Selected Dependent Variables

A.5.1 (TERMS OF ADDRESS OMITTED)

A: The employees that are under your supervision, I believe that they, uh, work with a live current?

I: ¿Entiendo que los trabajadores que trabajan bajo su supervisión trabajan con la corriente viva?

W: Eso es correcto.

I: That is correct.

A: And is it your office and your employees and yourself those that are in charge of, uh, providing maintenance and security to the switching unit where the accident occurred?

I: ¿Y entiendo que es su oficina, sus empleados y usted quienes le dan mantenimiento y e—examinan las unidades de, eh, eh, de los tr—, eh, donde occurió el accidente?

W: ¿Podría repetir la pregunta?

I: Could you repeat the question?

A: Okay it is the employees and yourself that are in charge of providing—of making sure that the switching units where the accident occurred are properly secured?

I: ¿Y es usted y los—y sus empleados los que se ocupan—están a cargo de que esté correctamente—de que esté de una forma segura los transformadores donde occurió el accidente—de la seguridad de los transformadores?

W: Bueno, la técnica de C—región C, eh, entiendo el pueblo de C como tal sí. No exactamente donde occurrió el accidente, sino toda el área de C como tal.

I: The technical unit provides a—for the whole area of C, not exactly to that spot, but to the whole city of C.

A: But of course *sir*, we know that the switching unit where the accident occurred is located in C.

I: Pero claro, sabemos que los transformadores donde occurrió el accidente están en C.

W: Sí, pero no exactamente. O sea, en el momento del accidente yo estaba en la sección de—de, estuve en sección de soterrado. Ahora mismo yo no estoy en sección de soterrado.

I: Yes, you see but exactly at that time I was working on the unde—underground unit. Right now I am not working on the underground unit.

A: *Sir* at the time of the accident if there was no padlock in the door of a switching unit like this one, it would be your office that will be in charge of going there and placing the padlock?

I: ¿Digamos como al momento del accidente si no hay un candado en el transformador como este sería la responsabilidad de la oficina de usted y de asegurarse y poner un—un candado?

W: Sí, mía y de cualquier cuidadano responsable.

I: Yes mine and—and of any responsible citizen.

A: Yeah, and I am talking about you, because you are an employee of the P. *Sir* I am not talking about any other citizen. It is your responsibility as an employee of the P to make sure that that switching unit is properly secured. It's a simple question, yes or no?

I: Es una pregunta muy sencilla que requiere que conteste si o no. No estamos hablando de cualquier cuidadano sino que la responsabilidad suya o de cualquier otro empleado de P es asegurarse que esa unidad esté en condiciones seguras y que tiene su candado, ¿si o no?

W: Eso es así.

I: That's correct.

A: Okay. Uh, Mr. N. you know, uh, as you can see I'm showing here you what's been marked as plaintiff's exhibit number 1, uh, do you recognize what's reflected in that exhibit *sir*?

I: Le muestro lo que ha sido marcado exhibit uno de la parte demandante, ¿reconoce usted lo que aparece ahí en ese exhibit?

W: Sí.

I: Yes.

A: That is the switching unit that is located at the B.K. at the parking lot of the B K. of I.V., is that correct?

I: Ese es el transformador que se encuentra localizado en el estacionamiento del B.K. en I.V., ¿no es cierto?

W: Ese es un switche.

I: That's a switch.

A: A switching unit. Yes.

I: Lo que dicen "switching unit."

W: Sí.

I: Yes.

W: Una unidad seccionalizadora.

I: We call it in Spanish unidad seccionalizadora, "switching unit."

A: Okay. ¿Mr. N., eh, you are aware that March 21st, 1999 a child was involved in an accident in this particular switching unit that is reflected in plaintiff's exhibit number 1?

I: ¿Usted está al tanto, no es cierto señor N., que el 21 de Marzo del año 99 un niño estuvo involucrado en un accidente que occurrió en esta unidad seccionalizadora que aparece aquí?

W: Eso es correcto.

I: That's correct.

A: Now, ¿*sir* at some time in the afternoon of March the 21st, 1999 you were present at the parking lot of the B.K.?

I: ¿Y es cierto o no que en la tarde del 21 de Marzo del 99 usted estuvo presente en el estacionamiento del B.K.?

W: Eso es correcto.

I: That's right.

A.5.2 (POLITENESS OMITTED)

A2: Officer V. you have investigated many cases for the, uh, P, correct?

I: Señor V. usted ha investigado muchos casos para P, ¿no?

W: Correcto.

I: Correct.

A: How long have you been investigating cases for *P*?

I: ¿Cuánto hace que está investigando casos para *P*?

W: Alrededor de 11 años.

I: About 11 years.

A: In those 11 years investigating cases, you have become aware of, uh, problems, uh, in switching units regarding corrosion, lack of padlocks, and open doors, is that correct?

I: ¿Y durante ese tiempo usted se ha dado cuenta y ha visto problemas en las unidades seccionalizadoras de corrosión, de que no tienen los candados, y puertas abiertas?

W: Correcto.

I: Correct.

A: And you also have seen those problems specifically in schools, fast food restaurants, and housing projects, correct?

I: ¿Y había visto usted, específicamente, esos problemas en escuelas, en lugares de comida rápida, y en—en, proyectos, o sea en, en vivienda pública?

W: Sí. Tengo conocimiento de ello.

I: Yes. I have knowledge of that.

A: In fact you have testified as a witness in several complaints concerning these allegations, is that correct?

I: ¿Y de hecho ha testificado usted como perito en varios casos alegando estos—estas situaciones?

W: Sí, correcto.

I: Yes, correct.

A: Eh, in none of those cases as, uh, P recognizes there were any problems with the, with the switching units, is that correct?

I: Y en ninguno de esos casos ha admitido P que había problemas con las unidades seccionalizadoras, ¿correcto?

[Objection]

A: Okay. So you and P were aware of those prior complaints, is that correct?

I: Así que usted y P estaban al tanto—sabían que existían estas quejas o demandas anteriores, ¿correcto?

W: No entiendo la pregunta con respecto a quejas anteriores.

 I: I do not understand the question as to prior complaints.

A: Okay. Let me ask again. Were you aware of any complaints against P?

I: ¿Estaba usted al tanto de algunas demandas que habían sido radicadas anteriormente de los hechos de este caso en contra de P?

W: Sé de una en particular de niños con candado—con fue, este, con la unidad abierta sin candado.

I: I know specifically about one, of children with the door of the unit open without a padlock.

A: Can you *please* tell us about that case?

I: ¿Puede hablarnos de ese caso?

W: De ese caso, este, el caso se transó.

I: About that case, you see the case was settled.

A: And do you remember who were the parties in that case?

I: ¿Recuerda quiénes eran las partes en ese caso?

W: Permítame un segundo.

I: If you give me a second.

W: La demandante era A.B..

I: A.B. was the plaintiff.

A: And the—what was the date of that accident?

I: ¿Y la fecha de ese accidente?

W: El año fue en el 1991.

I: The year was 1991.

A: How old was the child involved in that accident?

I: ¿Qué edad tenía el niño involucrado en este accidente?

W: No recuerdo.

I: I don't recall.

A: Okay. *Thank you.* And do you remember what was the allegation in that complaint?

I: ¿Y recuerda cuál era la alegación de esa demanda?

W: Se alegaba en la demanda que la madre iba con el niño caminando por una acera,

I: It was alleged in that case that the mother was walking with the child on a sidewalk.

W: Y desconocemos como sucedió. El niño entró a la unidad seccionalizadora y tuvo un contacto eléctrico,

I: And we don't know how it happened. The child entered the switching unit and the child had an electric con—contact.

W: La unidad—la unidad no tenía candado. Estaba—estaba abierta.

I: The unit did not have a padlock. It was open.

A: Okay. And that's the only complaint you're aware of? That you remember?

I: ¿Y esa es la única demanda que usted se acuerda—de la que se acuerda?

W: Eh, de gabinetes abiertos sin candados, la única.

I: Of open cabinets without padlocks, the only one.

A: Okay, uh, I want to show the witness exhibit 54 line 47 dash six.

I: Le quiero mostrar el exhibit 47 raya seis.

A: I'm sorry identification 47 dash six.

I: No es exhibit—identificación 47 raya seis.

[Objection]

A: Mr. V. that complaint that you have there is of L.M. vs. Housing Department and P and others. That is an accident that occurred on December 2nd, 1998.

I: Ese documento que usted tiene ante usted es una demanda presentada por L.M. contra el departamento de la vivienda y la autoridad de X, por hechos que occurrieron el 2 de diciembre.

[Judge asks for clarification about the type of document].

A: Mr. V., do you recognize this document?

I: Sr. V. ¿Reconoce este documento?

W: Sí. Correcto.

I: Yes. Correct.

A: Mr. V. this is one of the documents that you personally produced Mr. I. as part of discovery, isn't this correct?

I: ¿No es cierto que ese es uno de los documentos que usted personalmente le
   entregó al licenciado Izquierdo como parte del descubrimiento de este
   caso?

W: Correcto.

I: Correct.

A: And the request was to produce, uh, complaints that had to do with similar events to the one in this case?

[Objection as to leading; overruled]

I: ¿Y no es cierto que usted entregó este documento a petición nuestra de que
   sometiera demandas que tuvieran que ver con casos similares al que nos
   concierne?

W: Yo sometí los documentos con casos similares, pero de este caso, es de casos cerrados los cuales obtuvieron ustedes en la división legal,

I: I—I submitted documents of similar cases, but this is a case that is closed
   and you obtained this case from the legal division.

W: Lo sometido fue a petición de ustedes y ustedes identificaron los casos.

I: What was submitted was by request of—of you and you requested the specific cases.

A: When you say division legal—legal division, was it the legal division of
   P?

I: ¿Y cuándo nos referimos a la división legal—se refiere a la división legal
   de P?

W: Correcto.

I: Correct.

A: To make it clear to the jury and to the judge this is something that you gave
   us?

I: ¿Para que este claro ante el juez y el jurado, esto fue algo que usted nos entregó a nosotros?

W: Correcto.

I: Correct.

W: Solicitado por ustedes.

I: Upon your request.

A: Can you read paragraph 11 please?

[Objection; overruled]

A: *Mr. V.* what were the, uh, could you read for us the allegations on paragraph 11 of that document?

I: ¿Nos puede leer las alegaciones en el párrafo?

[Judge's objection]

A: Now Mr. V., uh, you conducted an investigation of the accident in this
   case, correct?

I: Sr. V. usted llevó a cabo una investigación sobre el accidente en este caso, ¿correcto?

W: Correcto.

I: Correct.

A: When was that investigation made?

I: ¿Cuándo se llevó a cabo esa investigación?

W: ¿El día?

I: The date?

A: Yes.

I: Sí.

W: Eh, fue el 23—el martes 23. Creo que de marzo. El accidente fue el 21—el martes 23 durante la mañana.

I: It was on the 23—Tuesday the 23. The accident was Sunday the 21st, so this was Tuesday the 23rd in the morning.

A: *Thank you.* ¿What did you do as part of your investigation on Tuesday the 23rd?

I: ¿Qué hizo usted como parte de su investigación el martes 23—del martes 23?

W: Yo hice varias cosas.

I: I did several things.

A: Please tell us.

I: Díganos, por favor.

W: Eh, entre—yo concerté una cita primeramente con el supervisor de la Autoridad de X a cargo del soterrado en el distrito de C.

I: I, uh, I got an appointment with the supervisor of the electric company in charge of the underground system in the district of C.

A: Who was that?

W: El nombre de él era B.N.—el nombre de el es B.N.

I: His name is B.N.

A: What did you do next?

I: Luego, ¿qué hizo?

W: Como parte de la investigación, pues, yo fui al lugar a ver, a tratar de indetificar el lugar del contacto eléctrico del menor en este caso—

I: As part of the investigation I went to the place—the site in which this occurred, and tried to identify the place when this minor had the contact with the electricity—

W: —Y a entrevistar a las personas, eh, que residieran en el lugar o que trabajaran en el lugar. Que conocieran de los hechos.

I: And also to interview people who lived around the area or worked around the area who had knowledge of the facts.

A.5.3 (DISCOURSE MARKERS OMITTED)

A: Mrs. V., this sworn statement was given by you just hours after the incident, was it not?

I: ¿No es cierto que esta declaración jurada se le dio a usted unas horas después del accidente?

W: Eso es correcto.

I: That's correct.

A: Now the first part that you said that the officer told you that someone had called to report an act X, that's correct?

W: Correcto.

I: Correct.

A: And you told him that everything was fine.

I: Y usted le dijo que todo estaba bien.

W: Eso es corecto.

I: That is correct.

A: Now, the second incident or fact of that point there is you got into the car, and the officer or the policeman or the cop told you not to leave. Got out of the car and told you not to leave.

W: Correcto.

I: Correcto.

A: And when he asked why, the cop said that they had to do the work because he was upset—"alterado."

I: Y él—lo siguiente es que ellos le dicen a usted que tenían que arrestarlo. Entonces usted le preguntó porqué. Y el policía—un policía le dijo porqué ellos tenían que hacer su trabajo y porqué *J* estaba alterado, eh, eh, ¿eso es correcto?

W: Eso es correcto.

I: Uh, that's correct.

A: The next incident that you stated is that they threw him down to the floor and hit him with something that looked like a sword that was round on the tip?

I: ¿El siguiente incidente que usted dice que occurrió fue que lo tiraron al piso y le dijo—y le dieron, eh, con una espada que la punta es redonda?

W: Correcto.

I: Correct.

A: *Then* the next thing that you say there is that they arrested him.

I: Y después lo siguiente que usted dice es que lo arrestaron.

W: Correcto.

I: That's correct.

A: And the next thing you say, finally, is that they put him in the patrol car.

I: Y lo último que usted dice es que lo—lo pusieron—lo montaron en una patrulla.

W: Correcto.

I: Right.

A: Those facts at that time when you gave this sworn statement were clear in your mind, where they not?

I: ¿No es cierto que cuando usted dio esta declaración jurada los acontecimientos que habían occurido esa noche los tenía frescos en su mente.

W: Eso es correcto.

I: That's correct.

A: ¿So when J got hit, find that you say in this sworn statement, he had already been scoffing with the cops—resisting arrest?

I: ¿De manera que cuando J empieza, le da a un policía? [A: NO, when J got hit by a police officer]. ¿Cuando un policía le dio a J, eh, ya J había, eh, estado en un forcejeo?

W: Eso es correcto.

I: That is correct.

A: And when J got hit all the patrol—all the back up had already arrived there?

I: ¿Y cuando le golpearon a J ya todo los refuerzos de la policía y las patrullas estaban alli?

W: Sí, estaban allí. Pero antes de eso el oficial que lo saca del carro,

I: Yes they were there, however, before that, the officer that pulled him out of the car.

W: Que fue el alto lo había sacado—cuando él lo sacó del carro lo había tirado al piso,

I: It was the tall one, when he pulled him out of the car and threw him to the ground.

W: Ahí fue que él se trató de parar,

I: It was at that point when he tried to stand up.

W: Y zafarse del guardia,

I: And release himself from the officer.

W: Y ahí fue que ocurrió eso.

I: And then—then. At that point that happened.

A: *Alright. Now* let me ask you a couple of things, were all your friends standing around when all of this was going on?

I: Le voy a preguntar una cosa, ¿todas sus amistades estaban allí en el lugar mientras todo esto estaba ocurriendo?

W: Cuando empezaron a arrestar a J—

I: When they started, uh, arresting J—

W: —Ellos se fueron.

I: They left.

A: So up to that moment they all—all of them were around.

I: ¿O sea, que hasta ese momento entonces todos ellos estu—estuvieron alli?

W: Bueno, se bajaron del carro y estaban preguntando porqué le estaban haciendo eso.

I: Well they did get out of their cars and they were asking him why he was doing that.

A: So they were interacting with the police also?

I: ¿O sea también estaban interactuando con la policía?

W: Bueno estaban preguntándole.

I: Well they were asking the questions.

A: *Now*, you said that in this, uh, at this time also other people were coming down to leave.

I: Usted dijo que cuan—que en ese momento otras personas estaban saliendo para marcharse de allí.

W: Correcto.

I: Correct.

A: Did they remain around in the area to look at what was going on?

I: ¿Se quedaron allí para ver lo que estaba pasando?

W: Esas personas, vuelvo y repito, se fueron.

I: I—I—I repeat those people left.

A: *So* they saw all this incident. I'm sorry. Let me ask you this, were they able to from where they were standing—from where THEY were standing, where they able to see what was going on?

I: ¿Estas personas podían ver desde el lugar donde estaban—podían ver lo que estaba occuriendo?

A: When they got the—out of the house?

I: ¿Cuándo salieron de la casa?

W: Bueno, si miraban hacia donde está el altercado,

I: Well, if they—if they looked towards the place where the incident was taking place.

W: Se podía ver.

I: They could see it.

A: *Okay*. So they saw cops around, people around, some friends that have been in the party, but they left. That's your an—your testimony?

I: ¿O sea, usted lo que dice es que lo vieron personas ahí, policías, y se fueron—se fueron de ahí?

W: Eso es correcto.

I: That's correct.

A: *Now*. You told us that there had been alcohol in the party, did you drink?

I: Usted nos dijo que en la fiesta hubo alcohol, ¿usted bebió—bebió?

W: Yo no bebo.

I: I don't drink.

A: Did, uh, your friends drink?

I: ¿Y sus amistades bebieron?

A: The ones that came in your car?

I: Las que estaban en su carro?

W: The girls?

I: ¿Las muchachas?

W: Las muchachas no.

I: Not the girls.

A: The other three people that you mentioned yesterday, but you didn't recall their names, did they drink?

I: Y las tres—y las tres personas que usted mencionó ayer pero sus nombres no recordó, ¿esas personas ingirieron alcohol?

W: ¿Las muchachas?

I: The girls, are you asking?

A: Well, you mentioned one name who was a driver. Who was that? What was his name? Could you tell the members of the jury the name of this person?

I: Usted mencionó el nombre del conductor. ¿Quién era ese? ¿Cómo se llamaba? Dígale a los miembros del jurado el nombre de esta persona?)

W: J.

I: J.

A: *So* you mentioned J, but you told us yesterday that you didn't recall the other three person's names, did they drink?

I: Usted mencionó a J, pero ayer nos dijo que no podía recordar los nombres de est—de esas tres personas. ¿Esos tres bebieron?

W: No.

A: So no one driving in the car from 10 to 2:30am drank in that party?

I: ¿O sea que entre las 10 de la noche y las 2:30 de la mañana ninguna de las personas que llegaron en—en ese mismo auto inger—bebie—bebieron?

W: Bueno yo—yo—yo las vi bebiendo refrescos pero no bebiendo alcohol.

I: Well, I—I saw them drinking soft beverages, but I did not see them drink any alcohol.

A: Now, what about M, was he drinking?

I: ¿Ahora M bebió—estaba bebiendo?

W: Èl, creo que se bebió como una—dos cervezas.

I: I believe that he had one—two beers.

A: What about R, did he drink?

I: ¿R bebió?

W: Lo que yo vi, no.

I: Not from where I saw.

A: What about L, did he drink?

I: ¿Y L bebió?

W: Èl se bebió un vasito de limonsillo, pero eso le cayó mal y él no quiso beber más.

I: He had uh, uh, a glass of limonsillo, but he didn't want to drink any—anything else.

A: Could you explain what that is?

I: ¿Podría explicar lo que es limonsillo?

W: Eh, eh, tiene, mm, Bacardí limón,

I: It has Bacardi and lemon, uh, Bacardi with uh rum.

W: Agua,

I: Water.

W: Y Crystal Light.

I: And Crystal Light.

A: Okay. And what about A, did he drink?

I: Okay. ¿Y A bebió?

W: Que yo lo haya visto no, porque él estaba con su esposa y él no estaba,

I: Not that I, uh, I didn't see him drink, because he was with his wife and he was.

A: What about C, did he drink?

I: ¿Y C bebió?

W: Creo que se bebió dos cervezas también.

I: I think that he too had two beers.

A: What about F, did he drink?

I: ¿Y F bebió?

W: C/F es la misma persona.

I: C/F is the same person.

A: Thank you. And L and J are the same also?

I: ¿Y L y J son la misma persona?

W: L y J, sí.

I: L/J, yes.

A: *Alright. Now*, of these ten people that arrived in those two cars the person who drank the most had 2 beers in all that time during that party?

I: ¿De todas las personas que llegaron allí en ese auto, eh, se tomaron dos cervezas entre las 10:00 y las 2:30 de la mañana?

W: Todas las personas no.

I: Not all the people.

A: I'm talking about those ten that we talked about right now.

I: Me refiero a esos diez,

A: I'm sorry, those—those nine, because I haven't mentioned J.

I: Eh, esos nueve de los cuales hemos hablado. No son diez porque todavía no he mencionado a J.

W: *So* the—the one that drank the most had two beers—had two beers.

I: La persona que más bebió lo más que se tomó fueron dos cervezas.

W: Eso es correcto. Nosotros no acostumbramos a beber cuando salimos.

I: That is correct. We are not in the habit of drinking when we're—when we go out.

A: Now what about J, did he drink?

I: Ahora ¿J bebió?

W: J bebió una cerveza y un vasito de limonsillo.

I: Uh, J had one beer and, uh, a cup of limonsillo.

A: *Now* you said that the police officer ignored you when you were going to give him—to give him the information?

I: ¿Usted dice que el policía la ignoró cuando usted fue a darle la información?

W: Correcto.

I: Correct.

A: Isn't it true that he ignored you because he was keeping an eye on all the people that were around?

I: No es cierto que él la ignoró porque él estaba vigilando—velando, eh, a todas las personas que estaban en el sitio?

W: Yo no sé si él estaba pendiente a las personas que estaban en el sitio.

I: I don't know whether he was looking at the people who were at the place.

W: Sólo sé que si yo estoy hablando con alguien tengo que atenderlo.

I: All I know is that if I am speaking, uh, if I am talking to someone I have to pay attention.

A: Now, does J have any hearing problems?

I: Ahora ¿J, eh, tiene algún problema de—con la audición?

W: No.

I: No.

A: *Now* you testified yesterday that you could hear what he was talking, uh, by the car that you had arrived in with a cop while he was talking in a normal voice.

I: Usted dijo que cuando usted estuvo hablando con el policía, eh, en el carro en que usted llegó él estaba en un tono normal.

W: ¿Repítame la pregunta?

A: Sure.

I: Repeat the question

A: Sure—sure. Did you hear the conversation between J and the police officer?

I: ¿Usted pudo oír la conversación entre J y el policía?

W: El—que yo había escuchado al oficial a él no le dijo nada. El simplemente lo agarró y lo sacó del carro.

I: That I have heard—that I heard nothing. All he did was—the officer did was grab him and pull him out of the car.

A: So you didn't hear J asking why are you arresting me and J saying I want to talk to L? You didn't hear any of those things then?

I: ¿De manera, entonces, que usted en ningún momento escuchó a J decir porque lo estaban—le estaban haciendo eso que también él quería hablar con usted, eh, con L?

W: Okay. Usted me preguntó,

A: My question is, did you hear that?

I: ¿La pregunta es si usted escuchó eso?

W: Recuerde que,

[Judge interrupts]

W: Okay. Sí, yo lo escuché.

I: Okay. Yes, I did hear him.

A: And he was talking at that time in a normal voice?

I: ¿Y en ese momento, él estaba hablando, eh, en una voz normal?

W: Correcto.

I: Correct.

A: *So* would it be fair to say then that he could hear all the conversation that you had during those 15 minutes with the cop that was talking to you?

I: ¿Podríamos decir que él podía—pudo escuchar la conversación suya con el policía durante los 15 minutos que duró la conversación?

W: ¿Qué conversación?

I: What conversation?

A: The conversation that you had with the officer. That was asking for your information.

I: La infor—la conversación que tuvo con el policía cuando le estaban pidiendo la información.

W: ¿Quién escuchó?

I: Who heard?

A: Let me go back, because that was your testimony yesterday and maybe you forgot. Yesterday didn't you tell us that you were interacting with this cop that was asking you for information and you got several times into a car and out of the car talking, and you talked to him during that process?

I: ¿Ayer, uh, usted dijo que, se lo repito por si acaso se le olvidó, que usted estuvo interactuando con este policía y varias veces usted se montó en el auto, se salió del auto, se volvió a montar, se volvió a salir?

W: Eso es correcto.

I: That's correct.

A: *Now*, if *J* doesn't have any hearing impairment is it fair to say that he could hear from where he was?

I: ¿Si *J* no tiene impedimentos para poder oír bien podríamos decir que él la, eh, podía escucharla a usted de dónde—el lugar de dónde él estaba?

W: Podría ser.

I: It could be.

A: *Okay*. And that during that time you told us yesterday that he never went back there to talk to you and the police?

I: Usted dijo que durante este tiempo en ningún momento él fue allá para hablar con usted y la policía.

W: Eh, ¿J?

I: Eh, J?

A: Yes.

I: Sí.

W: No. Èl no llegó hasta donde yo estaba a hablar con la policía.

I: He did not come to the place where I was with the police officers.

A: And you explained yesterday that he didn't because he didn't realize that you—that the police was still there?

I: ¿Y ayer usted dijo que él no—él no llegó a hacer, porque él no se había dado cuenta de que la policía estaba allí?

W: Yo no dije que él no se había dado cuenta que la policía estaba allí—

I: I didn't—I didn't say that he had not realized that the police officers—officer was there—

W: —Yo lo que dije fue que cuando yo me monté en el vehículo y él se fue a su vehículo-

I: What I said was that when I got into my vehicle and he got into his vehicle—

W: —Eh, que el oficial le dio un cantazo y él no se dio cuenta—

I: He didn't see—realize that the cop hit him—

W: —Pero cuando yo estaba interactuando con el oficial—

I: However, while I was interacting with the police officer—

W: El otro oficial alto lo sacó del carro y él podía escuchar.

I: The other—the tall policeman pulled him out of the car and he could hear.

A: Didn't—didn't 15 minutes pass from the moment *J* moved towards his car and got into his car and the moment he was taken out of the car?

[Judge's objection]

A.5.4 (DISCOURSE MARKER *WELL* OMITTED)

A: And then what happened?

W: *Pues*, el oficial viene, me lo arrastra hasta la patrulla, y me lo tira dentro de la patrulla.

I: The officer came, he took him, he dragged him to the patrol car and dragged him into the patrol car.

A: And, uh, what did you do?

I: ¿Usted que hizo?

W: *Pues*, ellos se lo llevaron en la patrulla y allí había una persona, no lo conocía, y le pedí que por favor que me llevara a—al cuartel.

I: They took him away. There was someone there whom I didn't know and I asked him whether he could do me a favor and take me to the police station.

A: What did you observe before they took J into the patrol car, as far—as far as if there were any other police officers in the area?

I: ¿Y qué otra cosa usted vio cuando metieron a J en el carro, en terminos de los policías que había ahí?

W: No entendí la pregunta.

I: I didn't understand the question.

A: Uh, before they took J away, did you observe the presence of other police officers besides the ones that were involved in the incident that you described?

I: Antes de que se llevaran a J—antes de que se llevaran a J, usted llego a ver otros policías allí aparte de los que estaban agrediendo, agrediendo a J.

W: Después—después de que me levanto que ellos se llevaron a mi hermano veo alrededor que habían varios—varios guardias.

I: After I got up and they took my brother away, there were police officers in the area.

A: Okay. After the police took your brother away, where did you go?

I: Después que se llevan a su hermano, ¿hasta dónde usted fue?

W: *Pues*, le—le, esta persona, no la conozco, le pido que por favor de que me lleve,

I: I ask this person unknown to me, uh, to please take me—to please take me as a favor.

W: Y él amablemente me llevó hasta el cuartel.

I: And he kindly took me to the police station.

W: Me lleva al cuartel.

A: What—what did you observe at the police station?

I: ¿Qué fue lo que usted vio allí en el cuartel?

W: Yo—cuando yo voy al cuartel mi hermano esta, [unintelligible] al cuartel.

I: When I got to the police station my brother was in a cell at the police station.

A: Uh, was there, uh, could you please describe the condition that you saw J at that time?

I: ¿Podría describir la condición en la cual usted vio que estaba su hermano?

W: Esta completamente hinchada la cara,

I: His face was all swollen.

W: Muchos hematomas en todo su cuerpo, la espalda,

I: Many bruises all over his body, his back.

W: What about his shirt?

I: Shirt?

A: Shirt?

I: Y la camisa?

W: Rota.

I: Torn.

W: Sí lo arrastraron.

I: [Unintelligible] they dragged him.

A: And, uh, what did you do after you saw your brother?

I: ¿Y qué hizo usted después de ver a su hermano?

W: Le decía a los guardias de que por favor, esto se puede acabar vamos a hablar. Yo—

I: I started telling the officer, please this is something that we can, uh, talk about and work out—

W: —Ellos me dicen que ellos están cumpliendo con la ley.

I: And they answered that they were enforcing the law.

A: What did you do after you spoke to the other officers?

I: ¿Qué hizo usted después de haber hablado con los demás oficiales?

W: Le digo que si [pause], cuando veo a mi hermano así le digo que si quiere una pastilla para el dolor—

I: When I saw my brother's condition, I asked him whether he would like, uh, uh, a painkiller—

W: —Cuando salgo estoy a pie, no—no tengo donde llegar a un sitio a comprarle algo.

I: When I stepped out I, uh, I didn't have a car. I was on foot and there wasn't a store nearby where I could go and buy him something.

A: What happened thereafter?

I: ¿Qué pasó después?

W: Pues, me—me quedo en el cuartel—

I: Well, I stayed at the police station—

W: —Esperando ahí llega la mama de L—

I: While I was waiting L's mother arrives—

W: —El padrastro—

I: The stepfather—

W: —Y ahí el padrastro pregunta que si puede ver a mi hermano—

I: And the stepfather asks whether he could see my brother—

W: —Y que si le puede ofrecer una pastilla para el dolor—

I: And whether he could offer him a pill for the pain—

W: —Ellos, *pues*, le dicen que sí. El va lo ve. Le ofrece algo de comer porque ellos no le dieron asistencia médica en ningún momento,

I: They said yes. Then he went to see my brother and, uh, he had not been attended or fed at all. They had done nothing for him at all—

W: —El le trae un sandwich, un jugo—

I: He brought him a sandwich, some juice.

A.5.5 (DISCOURSE MARKERS ADDED)

A: Let me ask you this, uh, who—who was appointed to—to work as your assistant, secretary, when you where appointed Head Manager?

I: ¿Cuando a usted la nombran gerente a quiénes nombraron para ayudarla a usted?

W: A nadie.

I: No one.

A: Did, eh, eh, P, eh, always have a secretary?

I: ¿P siempre tuvo secretaria?

W: Mientras fue gerente de personal sí, que era yo.

I: As long as he was personnel manager yes. It was me.

A: So when, uh, you were appointed, who—who did the secretarial and clerical undertakings of the personnel and payroll department?

I: Entonces cuando a usted la nombran, ¿quién hace—quién hacía—quién estaba a cargo del trabajo de oficina de cobro y de personal en la oficina?

W: Yo.

I: I would.

A: Did you get a—a pay raise because of this, uh, double duty?

I: ¿Debido a este doble trabajo, a usted le dieron aumento de sueldo?

W: No señor.

I: No sir.

A: You were paid less than P?

I: ¿Le pagaban menos que a P?

W: Eh, perdone, exactamente me pagaron. Bueno ellos me hicieron un aumento a—yo ganaba creo que 700 algo. Me dieron el aumento hasta 900 y entonces,

I: *Well,* I was making 700 something and they gave me a small increase up to 900.

W: Pero no era el salario que ganaba M.P.

I: But it was not the salary M.P. was making.

A: Uh, what was your access to, mm, employee files when you were secretary and then a manager at the personnel and payroll department?

I: ¿Y cuál era el acceso suyo a los expedientes de los expedientes de los empleados cuando era secretaria y después gerente del departamento de personal?

W: El mismo.

I: The same.

A: Was it full access?

I: ¿Tenía acceso completo?

W: Completamente.

I: Full.

A: Can we have plaintiff's exhibit 9 please? Could you tell us Doña C, without going into the content of the document, what—what is this document?

I: ¿Nos puede decir Doña C, sin entrar en el contenido del documento, qué es esto?

W: Este era, eh, el papel que se utilizaba—la forma que se utilizaba cuando había algún cambio para el, eh, para cualquier empleado.

I: *Well* it was—this was the piece of paper or the form used whenever there was any change in the employee.

A: And where was this, uh, uh, uh, documents like this would be filed?

I: ¿Y dónde se encontraban—dónde se pueden encontrar estos documentos—como este dónde estaban?

W: Este—este—este—este papel—esta forma—este documento se preparaba y entonces se mandaba a la oficina de payrol, a nóminas, y luego después se regresaba de la oficina de nómina a la oficina de personal para ser archivado en el expediente del empleado.

I: *Well*, this paperwork or this piece of paper or this form was sent over to the payroll section and then after it was filed there it was sent back to the personnel section in order to be filed away in the record—the employee's records.

A: And would this record be in the employees' permanent file?

I: ¿Y esto estaría entonces en un emp, en un, eh, eh, un archivo para, eh, eh, permanente del empleado?

W: Sí señor.

I: Yes, sir.

A: Now we ask that this exhibit be admitted your honor.

A: Doña *C* could you tell me—now entering into the content of this document, what is the—what is the date of this document?

I: *Bueno* y ahora entrando en el documento que ya ha sido admitido, ¿qué fecha tiene?

W: Tiene la fecha de 1 de Febrero de 1989. Quiero aclarar un punto,

I: It has a date of February 1st, 1989.

W: Quiero aclarar un punto. Y es el siguiente, este, esta forma fue firmada por el señor G.V.—

I: There is a point I'd like to clarify. This form is signed by G.V.—

W: —Porque hay que recordar que yo estaba en la oficina del Sr. G.V. con el SR. J.L.—

I: Because you have to remember that I was at the office of *G.V.* with Mr. J.L.—

W: —Y en la oficina del señor G.V.—

I: And at the office of G.V.—

W: —Había esta forma—

I: There was this form—

W: Entonces, por eso es que aparece la firma del Sr. G.V. en este—en este personnel action form.

I: And that is why the signature of Mr. V appears in this personal—personnel action form.

A: What you're saying is that the meeting that you describe occurred between you, G.V., and Mr. L. on the same date that this document was fine, uh, signed?

I: ¿Usted quiere decir que entonces la—la—la reunión que usted describió allá entre el Sr. V, Sr. L, y usted había occurido en la misma fecha en que se firma este documento?

W: Sí, señor.

I: Yes, sir.

A: What personal action does this document reflect?

I: ¿Y qué acción personal—de personal refleja este documento?

W: Perdone, no entendí la pregunta.

I: I'm sorry, but I don't understand the question?

A: Yes. I want to know, the—the action that is reflected in this document.

I: Lo que quiere saber el licenciado es qué tipo de acción se refleja en este documento.

W: La acción que occurrió fue lo del cambio de salario y la aceptación de la posición de gerente de personal.

I: *Well*, the—the change—the change that occurred was the—the change of salary and the acceptance of the position of, uh, personnel manager.

A: Okay. The document reflects what was the position before the change and what was the position after the change. Could you please tell the members of the jury what was the position before and the salary before and the position after and the salary after?

I: El documento refleja también cuál fue la posición y salario antes y cuál fue la posición y salario después de la acción de personal. ¿Puede mencionar a los miembros del jurado cuál eran las dos?

W: Eh, el de secretaria de personal—

I: From personnel secretary—

W: —To personnel and payroll manager—

I: To personnel and payroll manager—

A: And the—the salary for the, uh, secretary?

I: ¿Y el salario de la secre—de secretaria?
W: Ciento setenta y cinco dolares por semana.
I: One hundred and seventy five dollars a week.
A: And the salary for the new position?
I: ¿Y el salario de la nueva posición?
W: Novecientos dollares por mes—
I: Nine hundred dollars per month—
W: —Y también $50 como un car allowance—
I: And also $50 a month as a car allowance—
W: —Que sería revisado—
I: Which would be reviewed—
W: —En enero de 1982—
I: In January of 1982.

A.5.6 (THE USES OF SPEECH DISFLUENCES)

A: *Uh, uh,* you were traveling in different cars and there were about 5 cars, right?
I: Iban en distintos carros. Habían como 5 carros, ¿verdad?
W: Sí.
I: Yes.
A: And what was the purpose of that meeting that you held with this people *on the mor—on the 21st of March, 1999?*
I: ¿Y cuál era el propósito? ¿Por qué era, *uh*, que se estaban reuniendo con esta gente el 21 de marzo del 99?
W: Pues, para salir de paseo.
I: Well, to go for a ride.
A: To go for a ride and, and also to meet somebody?
I: Para ir—
A: Later on.
I: ¿Para ir de paseo y para más tarde encontrarse con alguien?
W: Sí.
I: Yes.
A: *And where—and who* is that person that you were, *uh*, about to receive that day?
I: ¿Y quién era esa persona que iban a recibir ese día?
W: El primo de A.
I: A's cousin.
A: Is that L.V.?
I: ¿L.V.?

W: Sí, pero no sé el nombre.

I: Yes, but I don't know his name.

A: And where was it that you all met?

I: ¿Y dónde fue que se reunieron todos?

W: ¿Allá en el aeropuerto?

I: You mean at the airport?

A: No. No. You met, uh, *some—some—sometime* at 9:30, you told me?

I: Usted me dijo que se fue con una gente. ¿Como a las 9:30 no fue que me dijo?

W: Sí.

I: Yes.

A: And where was it that you met them?

I: ¿Y dónde fue que se encontraron?

W: Ahí. ¿En ese—a esa hora?

I: There. At that time?

A: Yes. When you first met them. On that date

I: Sí. Cuando primero se encontró con ellos en ese día, ¿don—dónde?

W: *Ah*. Nos encontramos en la autopista.

I: Uh, we met at the freeway.

A: Do you know *what—where* they were coming from?

I: ¿Sabe de dónde venían ellos?

W: Sí.

I: Yes.

A: Where from?

I: ¿De dónde?

W: Ellos venían de *P de—de* la casa de mi primo.

I: They were coming from *P* from my cousin's house.

A: What's your *school—education*?

I: ¿Qué educación tiene usted?

W: Cuarto año.

I: High School.

A: Do you work?

I: ¿*Y* trabaja?

W: No. Estudio.

I: No. I study.

A: What is it that you study?

I: ¿Y qué está estudiando?

W: Cosmetología.

I: Cosmetology.

A: Alright. So you met *at the—at the*, uh, *to—*was it at the toll plaza?

I: ¿Y dónde fue que se reunieron? ¿En el peaje?

W: Más o menos. Sí.

I: More or less. Yes.

A: The toll plaza where?

I: El peaje, ¿dónde?

A: Because there are different toll plazas on—*first of all, did—did—did they*—this toll plaza is one of the toll plazas on the—on the expressway to S.J. from P.

I: ¿Este peaje es uno de los peajes en el expreso a S.J. de P?

W: Sí.

I: Yes.

A: And in which one did you meet?

I: ¿Y en cuál de ellos fue que se reunieron?

W: En el de J.D.

I: The one in J.D.

A: And that's because you live in J.D., right?

I: Y eso es porque usted vive en J.D., ¿verdad?

W: Sí.

I: Yes.

A: Okay. Proceed. And what happened after that? *You met and—tell me what happened?*

I: ¿Y entonces díganos qué pasó después de eso, *se reu—se jun—se reunieron* y entonces que pasó?

W: Okay. Seguimos—

I: Okay. We kept going—

W: —Luego viajamos para C—

I: Then we went down to C—

W: —Fuimos al baño y eso—

I: We used the bathroom *and* such—

W: —Con los niños—

I: With the kids—

W: —Seguimos—

I: We kept going.

A: And you bought groceries there, right?

I: Y allí compraron cosas de comer, ¿verdad?

W: Sí.

[Objection from counsel, leading]

I: Yes.

A: So, okay. So you stopped in. Did you buy anything *at—at* the C stop?

I: Bien. *Eh*, cuando pararon en C, ¿compraron algo?

W: Comida—

I: Food—

W: — *Y* refrescos —

I: And — and refreshments.

A: Okay. And so from there where did you go to? Uh, first of all were you all traveling together like tailgating or separate cars. How was it?

I: Y todos iban juntos como en caravana, *eh, eh*, en carros distintos. ¿*cómo — cómo* era el arreglo?

W: Sí. Era detrás del otro.

I: Yes. One behind the other.

A: And who was the leader of that group of cars?

I: ¿Y quién era el líder de esos carros?

W: Este, A y R después.

I: A and then R.

A: And you mean A *the plaintiff N — Mr. N.*

I: ¿Y cuándo usted dice A se refiere al demandante, al Sr. N?

W: Yes. Sí.

I: Yes.

Appendix 6

Text of Interruptions and Semiconsecutive Interpreting

A.6.1 (INTERRUPTIONS)

A: Would you explain to the court what is the purpose of the FED? What you just made reference to in your testimony.

W: La FED es una agencia que regula el precio para la leche que producen los ganaderos. La FED establece un precio fijo que son 10 centavos por galón de leche fresca. Este es el precio que paga *X*. Nosotros pagamos 52 centavos.

I: The FED is an agency that regulates the price of milk that farmers produce. The FED establishes a price, which is 10 cents per gallon of fresh milk. This is what *X* pays. We pay 52 cents.

A: A true statement, a correct statement would be to say that, uh, the *F.E.D.* establishes a minimum price for milk to the farmers?

W: *Bueno, desde, alrededor del 2000 entiendo que ellos decidieron establecer un precio mínimo para la leche que producen—*

I: Well, since I believe around 2000, they decided to establish a minimum price for the milk that they produce—

W: —En quotas.

I: In quotas.

A: And, how long has that been in practice by now?

W: *Pues, el mínimo—el precio mínimo se compone de dos factores. Es un precio ponderado—*

I: Well, that the, uh, minimum price is comprised of the two factors. It is a ponderated price—

W: —El precio que pagamos nosotros o que tenemos que pagar nosotros por la leche fresca y el precio que paga *I* que son 10 centavos—

I: The price that we pay or have to pay for fresh milk and the price that *I* pays which is 10 cents.

Judge: For what? I'm sorry.

I: Set a fixed price for their production.

Judge: Okay. Thank you.

W: O sea, la— la— el— el precio ponderado en las dos.

I: In other words, the ponderated price of both of them.

A: And it is a weighted average from the price plants pay to farmers, which I think you mentioned was 62.08 cents?

W: Correcto.

I: Correct.

A: And the price paid by *I* for the same raw milk?

W: 10 centavos.

I: 10 cents.

A: Which is paid at 10 cents?

W: Correcto.

I: Correct.

A: Is that correct?

W: Correcto.

I: Correct.

A: And from then a minimum price— a minimum price that is going to be paid to the farmer?

W: Sí. Ese precio es siempre por debajo del precio que pagamos a las plantas.

I: Yes. That price is always under the price we pay the plants.

A: That price right now as you mentioned is 52 cents?

W: Cincuenta y dos centavos minimo.

I: Fifty-two cents minimum.

A: And you are paying 62.18 cents?

W: Correcto.

I: Correct.

A: Well, there's a difference right there.

W: *Correcto. A ellos se le paga diez centavos menos, porque, eh, la cantidad de leche que nosotros vendemos en el mercado no da para pagarles a ellos, eh, 62 centavos y—*

I: Correct. We pay them ten cents less, because the amount of milk that is sold in the market is not enough to pay them 62 cents.

A: When *X* is paying 62.18 and *I* is paying only ten cents, is that right? Correct?

W: Correcto. *I* paga diez centavos.

I: Correct. *I* pays ten cents.

A: Mr. *C.* You mentioned a little while ago that Mr. *A.B.* has now the position of executive director of el *F.E.D.* and is also the administrator of *I*. Uh, who used to pay Mr. *B*'s salary?

W: *El salario del Sr. B lo pagaba I—*

I: Mr. *B*'s salary was paid by *I—*

W: —Hasta Diciembre del año pasado—

I: Until December of last year—

W: —Donde el *F.E.D.* decidió que lo pagaría el *F.F.L.I.*.

I: Where the *F.E.D.* decided that the *F.F.L.I.* would pay for it.

A: Mr. *C* you mentioned a little while ago, uh, that there were about 350 farmers, uh, how much milk— raw milk, do these farmers produce annually?

W: *Bueno, nosotros utilizamos el— el— el litro como la medida de— de la producción de leche y—*

I: —We use the liter as the milk production measurement.

A.6.2 (SEMICONSECUTIVE INTERPRETING)

A: Did you, uh, conduct an evaluation of the plaintiffs?

W: Eso es correcto.

I: That is correct.

A: Did you reach an opinion as a result of that evaluation?

W: Eso también es correcto.

I: That is also correct.

A: Can you tell us please— can you tell the jury what that opinion is?

W: ¿En el caso de quién?

I: In which— in the case of whom?

A: As to, uh, *A.N.*

W: De *J.A.N.* Okay.

I: *J.A.N.* Okay.

W: *Los resultados de la evaluación psicológica que llevé a cabo—*

I: The results of the psychological evaluation that I performed—

W: *—En— en mayo. A principio de mayo del año 2000—*

I: In May, towards the beginning of May of the year 2000—

W: *—Eh, demuestran que el Sr., eh, eh, J.A., eh, N—*

I: Showed that Mr. *J.A.N.* —

W: *—Padece de un post-traumatic stress disorder—*

I: Uh, uh, has a post-traumatic stress disorder—

W: *—With anxiety and depression.*

A: What is— what is post-traumatic stress disorder? Can you explain that?

W: *—Post-traumatic stress disorder es una condición—*

I: Post-traumatic stress disorder is a condition—

W: —*Que está, eh, acuñada en el diagnostic and statistical manual of mental disorders—*

I: Which is included in the diagnostic and statistical manual of mental disorders.

W: —*Que es— es el libro especializado que se usa en psiquiatría y psicología—*

I: Which is a specialized book that is used in psychology and psychiatry—

W: —*Para definir las condiciones mentales y emocionales—*

I: To define mental and emotional conditions—

W: —*De las personas—*

I: Of people—

W: —*En la— la— la cultura de nosotros. En la cultura de los E.U. y hispana—*

I: In our culture. The culture of the U.S. and the Hispanic culture—

W: —*Eh, en un— es una definición técnica, un poco larga, que si usted quiere se la— se la leo completa—*

I: It is a technical definition. It is quite long. If you want to I can read it in its totality—

W: ¿*O quiere un resumen?*

I: Or do you want a summary?

A: Give us— explain to the jury what it is.

W: In a nutshell?

A: Yes.

W: *Eh, el— el— el desorden de stress post traumático—*

I: Post-traumatic stress disorder—

W: —*Es una condición que surge como consequencia—*

I: It's a condition that results as a consequence—

W: —*De un— de la presencia de un estresor bien terrible—*

I: Of the presence of a very terrible stressor—

W: —*En— sobre la conducta de una persona—*

I: Over the conduct of a person—

W: —*Esa persona como consequencia de recibir ese estresor tan fuerte—*

I: And the person as a result of receiving that terrible stressor—

W: —*Es tocado en la profundidad de su estructura psíquica—*

I: It's touched in the depthness of the person's psychic structure—

W: —*Eh, ocasionándole, eh, a ese nivel de profundidad—*

I: Causing the person at that level of depthness—

W: —*Eh, eh, angustia—*

I: Anguish—

W: —*Ansiedad—*

I: Anxiety—

W: —*Depression*—

I: Depresion—

W: —*Y sufrimiento emocional severo*—

I: And severe emotional suffering.

W: —*La persona que sufre de un*— *de un desorden de estrés post traumatic*—

I: The person who suffers from post-traumatic stress—

W: —*Cambia su personalidad*—

I: It changes his or her personality—

W: —*O sea que es muy difícilmente vuelva a ser como era antes de en-frentarse a ese estrés*—

I: Meaning that the person will not— rarely becomes the same person— goes back to being the same person the person was before facing that stress—

W: —*Puesto que casi a diario revive esas experiencias traumáticas*—

I: Since almost daily the person relives those traumatic experiences—

W: —*Tiene sueños y pesadillas con esa experiencia traumática*—

I: The person sleeps and has, uh, uh, nightmares regarding that traumatic experience—

W: —*Trata de evitar esa experiencia traumática*—

I: The person tries to avoid that traumatic experience—

W: —*Trata de no pensar en ella*—

I: Tries not to think about it—

W: *Para no sentirla*—

I: So as not to feel it—

W: —*Pero generalmente no puede*—

I: But in ge— in general the person cannot—

W: —*Si la persona está a merced de esa experiencia traumática*—

I: If the person is at the mercy of that traumatic experience—

W: —*Por lo tanto, esa experiencia traumática generalmente es, eh, cuando uno es víctima de un robo*—

I: In general that traumatic stress experiences when you are the victim of rob-bery—

W: —*De*— *de*— *de una violación*—

I: Rape—

W: —*De un*— *o uno es, este, un soldado de la guerra*—

I: Or when you are a soldier at war—

W: —*Y pasa por experiencias donde uno se enfrenta a la muerte*—

I: And go through experiences in which you face death—

W: —*O como el caso del matrimonio de N*—

I: Or like in the case of the *N* couple—

W: —*Ellos percibieron y se enfrentaron a una*— *a una experiencia*—

I: They were faced and were in the presence of an experience—

W: —*En cual su hijo A.J.* —

I: In which their child *A.J.* —

W: —*Sufrió de— del— de una explosión— de una explosión eléctrica*—

I: Suffered from an electrical explosion—

W: —*Que y, eh, cayó de— de, al piso de— desmayado*—

I: And fell and fainted to the floor—

W: —*Sufrió quemaduras extremas*—

I: Suffered extreme burns—

W: —*Y esa, él— él percibía esa experiencia*—

I: And to go through that experience—

W: —*Les ocasionó a ellos esa experiencia traumática*—

I: Caused them that traumatic experience—

W: —*En adición, hay muchísimos otros, eh, eventos traumáticos en la vida de tanto el Sr. N como de la Sra. N como consecuencia de esa explosión*—

I: In addition, as a consequence of that explosion there are numerous traumatic experiences—

W: —*Y si usted quiere se las enumero.*

A: Sure, can you tell us?

I: And if you want to— if you want to I can name them.

A: Can you tell us what those traumatic events are?

W: *Seguro.*

I: Sure.

W: *Eh, bueno la— la primera es la explosión*—

I: The first one is the explosion—

W: —*Eh, en la cual ellos se enfrentaron a— a pensaron en un momento que el niño se iba a morir*—

I: Which they faced and, uh, uh, as a matter of fact they thought for a minute that the child would die—

W: —*Y entonces tuvieron, se— se vieron enfrentados a la muerte de su hijo en ese momento*—

I: At that time, they faced their child's death—

W: —*La segunda experiencia fue cuando a el niño lo llevan en ambulancia al hospital esa noche*—

I: The second one is that evening when the child is taken to the hospital in the ambulance—

W: —*Y, eh, en— el niño es atendido en emergencias*—

I: And the child is taken care of in the emergency room—

W: —*Y allí, pues, eh, eh, eh, como consecuencia de la conversación con los médicos*—

I: And while there and as a result of the conversation with the doctors.

W: —*Ellos— tanto el Sr. N como la Sra. N, concluyen que su niño está en estado crítico—*

I: Mr. *N* as well as Mrs. *N* reached the conclusion that their child is in a critical state—

W: —*El que esté en un estado crítico de salud se convierte en una experiencia traumática para ellos—*

I: The fact that he is in a critical state of health becomes a traumatic experience for them-

W: —*Esa sería la segunda—*

I: That would be the second—

W: —*La tercera sería cuando el— el— los médicos le pide— le piden permiso para operarlo de emergencia—*

I: The third one is when the doctors ask them for permission to [pause] perform emergency surgery—

W: —*Y no le aseguran de que el niño va a salir vivo de la— de la operación—*

I: And they cannot assure them that the child will come out alive from surgery—

W: —*Para una pareja joven como ellos—*

I: For a young couple like them—

W: —*Que han sido— eran— son unos papás— unos padres bien apegados a su— a sus hijos—*

I: Who have been and are new parents and are very close to their children—

W: —*Y han— han invertido gran cantidad de energía emocional en sus niños—*

I: And who have invested a large, uh, amount of energy in their children—

W: —*Que le digan que su hijo va a ser operado y que no le aseguran que salga vivo de la operación—*

I: To be told that their child is going to be operated on and they cannot assure that the child will come out alive from surgery—

W: —*Eso constituye una experiencia traumática también—*

I: That constitutes also a traumatic experience—

W: —*Otra— otro evento traumático occurre varios días después—*

I: Another traumatic event occurs several days later—

W: —*Cuando por primera vez el Sr. y la Sra. N—*

I: When for the first time Mr. and Mrs. *N*—

W: —*Ven a su hijo en el— en el hospital, en— en— en el— en el intensivo—*

I: See their child in the hospital. In the intensive care unit—

W: —*El niño está con los ojos cerrados—*

I: The child has his eyes closed—

W: —*Sin— sin— sin movimiento—*

I: Without movement—

W: —*Quemado*—

I: Burned—

W: —*Eh, con un color bien oscuro que no es el color del niño*—

I: With a very dark color which is not the child's complexion—

W: —*El niño esta, eh, pegado a unos, eh, life, eh, support machines*—

I: He is— he is on some life support machines—

W: —*Eh, y, y ellos, pues, se quedan en— en— en, eh. El— el— el verlo de esa manera. El percibirlo de esa manera*—

I: And to see him that way— to perceive him that way—

W: —*Le ocasiona un shock emocional bien profundo*—

I: Causes them a very deep emotional shock—

W: —*Que es un estresor que también es una experiencia traumática para el-los*—

I: Which is a stressor that is also a traumatic experience for them—

W: Eh—

A: Any other traumatic experiences that would—

W: Sí.

A: Trigger post-traumatic stress disorder?

W: La próxima—

I: Yes—

W: —*La experiencia traumática es cuando los médicos le piden permiso*—

I: The next traumatic experience is when the doctor asks them for permission—

W: —*Al Sr. y a la Sra. N*—

I: Mr. and Mrs. *N*'s permissions—

W: —*Para cortarle el brazo*—

I: To cut his arm—

W: —*Para el Sr. y la Sra. N eso fue una experiencia horrible*—

I: For Mr. and Mrs. N this was a horrible experience—

W: —*Porque, por un lado, ellos tenían que autorizar que le cortaran el brazo*—

I: Because, on the one hand, they had to authorize that the arm be cut—

W: —*O enfrentarse a otras consecuencias peores*—

I: Or face other worse, uh, consequences—

W: —*Como por ejemplo que el niño se fuera en una crisis*—

I: As for example that the child could go into a crisis—

Appendix 7

Texts of Nine or Fewer Words and Ten or More Words

A.7.1 (NINE OR FEWER WORDS)

A: *Did you go before or at the fifth day?*
I: ¿Fue usted antes o al quinto día?
W: *Antes del quinto día.*
I: Before the fifth day.
A: And you said that these documents were given to another person?
I: ¿Y usted dice que estos documentos le fueron entregados a otra persona?
W: *Correcto.*
I: Correct.
A: *And that person was working with those documents?*
I: ¿Y esa persona trabajaba con estos documentos?
   W: *Correcto.*
I: Correct.
A: Now, Mrs., ah, G., don't you go each day to the office of the commissioner to obtain the attendance sheets of the employees and return them in the afternoon?
I: Bien, señora G., ¿no es cierto que usted acude todos los días a la oficina del comisionado para solici—para procurar las hojas de asistencia de los empleados y luego las entrega?
W: NO.
I: NO.
A: *Was your office fixed?*
I: What?
A: *Was the office space that was given to you fixed?*
I: ¿El espacio de oficina que se le entregó fue arreglado?

W: Me cambia, uh, la última vez que estuve en una oficina que era como un tipo de cobacha—

I: The last time that I told you—what I told you was sorta like a storage room.

W: *—Nunca lo arreglaron.*

I: They never fixed it up.

W: Estoy en otra oficina al lado de ese—de esa oficina. De esa cobacha.

I: I'm in another office by the side, next to that office. To that, uh, storage room.

A: So then you were transferred from one office to another?

I: ¿Fue trasladada de una oficina a otra?

W: Después de haber estado en diferents oficinas,

A: Would you answer the question? That office that you were placed in, is that for the new position?

I: Y en esa oficina donde la colocaron,

[Objection].

A: Is that office that you were placed, after being—the office—the office that you are working now, when were you placed there?

I: La oficina donde usted actualmente trabaja, ¿cuándo fue enviada ahí?

W: *La fecha exacta no la recuerdo.*

I: I don't remember the exact date.

A: *Were you there by, ah, September 2001?*

I: ¿Se encontraba ahí para Septiembre del 2001?

W: *Pudo ser Septiembre.*

I: It may have been in September [W: Pudo ser]. It may have been.

A: Now that office were you are located right now, since around September 2001, over a year ago, is that in good condition?

I: ¿Y en esa oficina donde usted ahora mismo se halla, desde septiembre primero, hace más de un año está en buenas condiciones?

W: *Sí, porque yo la mantengo.*

I: Yes, because I keep it that way.

A: *Does it have a desk?*

I: ¿Tiene un escritorio?

W: *Sí.*

I: Yes.

A: *Does it have air?*

I: ¿Tiene aire?

W: *Sí.*

I: Yes.

A: Did it have air before or was it placed for you?

I: ¿Tenía un aire antes o se lo instalaron?

W: *Lo tenía antes.*

I: It had one before.

A: *And all the offices there have air?*

I: ¿Y todas la oficinas ahí cuentan con aire?

W: *Excepto una que no tiene aire.*

I: Except for one that does not have any air.

A: *Now, where you given, uh, an orthopedic chair?*

I: Bien, y le dieron una silla ortopédica?

W: *Sí.*

I: Yes.

A: *You requested that chair?*

I: ¿Usted solicitó esa silla?

W: *El F—el F—*

A: Could you answer that question?

W: *Sí, uh—*

I: YES.

W: *Con una—una—*

I: YES—

W: *Especificación.*

I: With a specification—

W: *De la C.F.S.E.—*

I: Issued by the S.I.F.

A: When you were placed in that office, did that office have telephone lines?

I: Cuando la instalaron en esa oficina, ¿tenía linea telefónica?

W: *No.*

I: No.

A: *Was it placed later?*

I: ¿Se instaló posteriormente?

W: *El teléfono.*

I: The phone.

W: *Lo llevé yo.*

I: I took it.

A: *I'm sorry, I asked about a telephone line.*

I: No, lo siento. Yo pregunto por una línea telefónica.

W: *Había línea telefónica, pero no había teléfono.*

I: There were phone lines, but there was no phone.

A: *Okay. So you have a telephone there?*

I: Entonces, ¿tiene un teléfono ahí?

W: *Eh, un teléfono sí. Y un teléfono que yo compré con mi dinero propio.*

I: YES a telephone. A telephone that I bought with my own money.

A: Haven't you also had a negative attitude since your transfer to the municipal police?

I: ¿No es cierto que usted también tiene una actitud negativa desde que fue trasladada de la policía municipal?

W: *No.*

I: No.

(Interruption. Attorneys approach the bench).

A: Now, Mrs. G, by 2001 who did you believe was performing your duties?

I: Bien, Sra. G., para el 2001, ¿quién entendía usted desempeñaba sus deberes?

W: *¿En qué lugar?*

I: Where?

A: The duties that you were supposed to be assigned.

I: Los deberes que se suponía se le hubiesen asignado.

(Objection)

A: Was anyone doing administrative assistant duties that would have—that should have been assigned to you in the recycling office?

I: ¿Habi—hubo alguien desempeñando deberes de asistente administrativa, uh, desempeñando deberes, perdone, que usted debió de haber estado desempeñando, uh, de asistente administrativa en la oficina de reciclaje?

W: *No.*

I: No.

A: Was there uh, anyone performing those duties at the municipal police?

I: ¿Había alguien desempeñando esos deberes en la policía municipal?

W: *No.*

I: No.

A: *No, ah, what about the human resources office?*

I: ¿Y en recursos—en la oficina de recursos humanos?

A: Was in 2000, was there anyone performing the duties as administrative assistant that you could have performed there?

I: En el 2001, había alguien que,

A: Uno. Two thousand (2000).

I: Dos mil (2000), eh, ¿había alguien que estaba desempeñando deberes de asistente administrativa que usted pudiese estar desempeñando?

(Objection).

A: Do you recall answering an interrogatory at the beginning of the discovery of this case?

I: ¿Recuerda usted haber respondido a un interrogatorio que se le presentó a principio de este caso?

W: Correcto.

A: And, uh, I'm going to show you this interrogatory dated November 17th 2001 and I am going to refer to you to answer 19.

I: Le voy a mostrar su interrogatorio fechado 12 de Noviembre del 2001 y deseo referirle a la contestación número 19.

A: Mrs. G, ah, since you have been at the municipal—municipal police performing the duties that you have been telling us about, you have been dealing with the attendance of the employees at the municipal police?

I: ¿Desde que usted estaba trabajando con la policía municipal desempeñando las funciones de las que usted está hablando, uh, usted está a cargo de la asistencia de los policías del municipio?

W: *Correcto.*

I: That is correct.

A: *And how many—around how many employees are there?*

I: ¿Como cuántos empleados hay?

W: *¿Policías Municipales?*

I: Municipal Police?

A: Employees that you—with whom you deal with—you manage attendance?

(Judge's interjection with regard to questioning style).

A: Do you deal with the attendance at the dependency of the municipal police?

I: ¿Usted, eh, maneja la—la—la, asistencia de la dependencia de la policía municipal?

W: *Sí. De los 18 policías municipales solamente.*

I: Yes. Of the only 18 municipal police.

A: *Did they work in shifts?*

I: ¿Trabajaban por turnos?

W: *Sí.*

I: Yes.

A: *How many shifts are there?*

I: ¿Cuántos turnos hay?

W: *Cuatro turnos.*

I: Four shifts.

A.7.2 (TEN OR MORE WORDS)

A: *Do you know where, if anywhere, was R.E.V. working prior to July 1ˢᵗ, 2002?*

I: ¿Sabe usted dónde, si acaso es así, que trabajó ella con antelación al primero de Julio del 2002? ¿Sabe usted dónde trabajó ella si acaso trabajaba con antelación al 1ro de julio?

W: *Entiendo que en el mantenimiento de la cancha bajo techo C.E., porque yo—porque ella trabajaba allí.*

I: It's my understanding that as a maintenance worker at the C.E. court, because she worked there.

A: *Do you know when, if at anytime, she started working for the municipality of S?*

I: ¿Sabe usted cuándo, si acaso así fue, que comenzó ella a trabajar para el municipio de S?

W: *Sinceramente no le se decir con exactitud pero desde—de principio porque ya cuando a mí me cambiaron a la cancha ya ellos estaban.*

I: Sincerely, I wouldn't be able to tell you, uh, with precision but it must have been from the very—very outset, because by the time I was—I got to the courtyard, uh, court, she was already there.

A: *When you say, uh, from the very outset to what period do you refer? To the outset of what?*

I: Cuando usted se refiere desde el principio, ¿se refiere al principio de qué?

W: Cuando comenzó el partido X,

I: When,

W: Y ejerció, este, comenzó el nuevo alcalde.

I: When the party started out and exercised. In other words, when the mayor started out?

A: What mayor?

I: ¿Qué alcalde?

W: A.L.M.

I: A.L.M.

A: Do you know R.L.R.'s political affiliation?

I: ¿Conoce la afiliación política de R.L.R.?

W: Sí.

I: Yes.

A: What is her political affiliation, if any?

I: Cuál es,

W: X.

I: She's an X.

A: *Do you know Ms. C.M.? Number 2 in the list of people identified as plaintiff's exhibit 11. C.M., do you know her?*

I: ¿Conoce usted a C.M.? Aparece número 2 en la lista que figura o consta en la prueba instrumental número once de los demandantes. ¿La conoce a C.M.?

W: Sí, la conozco.

I: Yes I know her.

A: Do you know her political affiliation?

I: ¿Conoce su afiliación política?

W: Sí, es X.

I: Yes she's an X.

A: *Do you know L.G. number 42 in that list marked as exhibit 11?*

I: ¿Conoce a L.G. el número 42 en la lista?

W: Sí.

I: Yes.

A: Do you know her—his political affiliation?

W: Sí, es X.

I: Yes he's an X.

A: *Mrs. D.S. when you said that you participated in the ceremony of taking office of the mayor, weren't you at that time acting director of the public relations office?*

I: Sra. D.S. cuando usted afirma que participó en la ceremonia de toma de posesión de juramento del alcalde, ¿no se desempeñaba usted como subdirectora interina de dicha oficina?

A: No, acting director.

I: Directora interina de esa oficina.

W: Sí, yo [unintelligible].

I: Yes, I was acting director.

A: Because, uh, Mrs. M.C., the director, was on vacation.

I: ¿Porque la Srta. M.C. estaba de vacaciones?

W: Eso es correcto.

I: That's correct.

A: *And, uh, she had—at that time had she resigned to her position?*

I: ¿Para ese momento había ya renunciado a su puesto?

W: *No, ella pidió disfrutar de sus vacaciones, o sea botar las vacaciones que le quedaban.*

I: No she asked permission to enjoy—in other words, uh, to use up her entire vacation leave.

A: But she did in fact resign to her position?

I: ¿Pero ella de hecho renunció a su puesto?

[Objection]

A: *Did you know that she resigned to her position as director?*

I: ¿Sabe usted—sabe usted si ella renunció a su puesto como directora?

W: *Bueno, entiendo que todo—que toda persona de confianza, ah, ah, cuando se va un alcalde tiene que renun—tiene que presentar su renuncia.*

I: Well, it's my understanding that everyone holding a trust position when the mayor leaves they have to resign.

W: Eso es parte de un protocolo a seguir.

I: That's part of a protocol that needs to be followed.

A: *But my question is, do you know if she did in fact resign?*

I: Pero mi pregunta es, si usted sabe—

W: *Yo desconozco. Yo no vi ningún documento, nada por el estilo.*

I: Well, I don't know. I saw no document or anything of the sort.

A: *Now, the public relations. When you in fact were performing some of the duties, uh, when the director was not there, didn't some of those duties entail representing the mayor in public activities?*

I: Bien. Cuando usted se encontraba como directora de relaciones públicas interina desempeñado algunos de esos deberes, ¿no es—no es cierto que, eh, usted en ocasiones representó al alcalde?

[Objection]

A: *Now, when you were performing those duties then you weren't, uh, taking the position of M.C. who was not at the office at that time?*

I: ¿Entonces usted cuando desempeñaba esas funciones, pues, estaba tomando, eh, pues, es cierta, eh, las funciones de M.C., que no se encontraba ahí?

W: Bueno, en parte sí. Claro que sí.

I: Well, in part yes. Of course.

A: Now, according to the stipulated facts by that time in—by that time in January of 2001 and since July 1, 2002 your position has been changed from typist clerk to office system administrator.

[Objection]

A: *Now, ah, system—office system administrator it's, uh, isn't that the name that in the municipality of S is given to what in other municipalities is called a secretary?*

I: Y bien una, eh, [short pause] una oficial administrativa de sistema computarizado no es, este,

A: De sistema de oficina.

I: De sistema de oficina, eh, ¿no es ese el título ocupacional que en otros municipios se le da a lo que comúnmente se llama secretaria?

W: Eso es correcto.

I: That's correct.

A: *So you, uh, by January, 2001 your position was of, I'm going to use secretary, but it was, uh, office system administrator?*

I: ¿Entonces desde el primero de junio del 2000 su título, voy a usar la palabra que no es, su título era secretaria o oficial administrativa de sistema de oficinas?

W: Eso es correcto.

I: That's correct.

A: *Were there other career employees with you in the public relations office?*

I: ¿Habían funcionarios de mayor rango en jerarquía que la suya en relacio—en relaciones públicas?

W: ¿En qué momento?

I: At what time?

A: By January 2001.

I: Para enero del 2001.

W: *En la oficina de relaciones públicas no había nadie de mayor rango que yo en aquel momento.*

I: At that time, at the public relations office no one else had a higher rank than mine.

A: Mr. E.L., wasn't he, uh, an assistant administrator?

I: El señor E.L.,

A: Administrative assistant.

I: ¿No era él un auxiliar administrativo?

W: Sí, eso es correcto.

I: Yes, that's correct.

A: Isn't that a higher-ranking position?

   I: ¿Y acaso ese puesto no es de mayor jerarquía?

W: *Si es de ma—mayor jerarquía, pero si van a un expediente él estaba bajo licencia de enfermedad.*

I: Yes it is a higher-ranking position, but if you go to the files you'll learn that he was on sick leave.

A: *Okay. So that by 2000—had he been working there in 2000?*

I: ¿Trabajó él ahí para el 2000 o alguien trabajó ahí?

W: Sí.

I: Yes.

A: What's that?

W: *¿Dos mil—después que el alcalde A.L.M. entra en posesión o antes?*

I: Meaning in the year 2000 after mayor A.L.M., uh, took office or before?

A: Hadn't it been around the time A.L.M. took office in January 2001?

I: ¿Pero acaso no fue en enero del 2001 que el alcalde A.L.M. ocupó su puesto?

W: Okay. Y como—para el 2000 estuvo allí trabajando.

I: Okay. Excuse me. In 2000, he was there. He was working there.

A: *Okay. So by 2000 M.C. is the director and E.L. was the administrative assistant and you were the secretary?*

I: ¿Entonces, pues, para el 2000 M.C. era la directora eh, eh, E.L. era el aux— el asistente administrativo y usted era la secretaria?

W: Eso es correcto.

I: That's correct.

A: *Now, you also told us that among the duties that you used to perform at public relations, uh, you used to give tours to visitors?*

I: ¿También mencionó que entre los deberes que usted desempeñaba en relaciones públicas usted le ofrecía excursiones al—los visitantes?

W: *Sí, eso es correcto. Le ofrecía excursiones a los visitantes, porque no hay ninguna plaza que diga guía turístico en—en—en—en—en el municipio de S y alguien tenía que hacerlo.*

I: Yes, that's correct I had to provide [unintelligible] tours to visitors because in the municipality of S there is no occupational position with the title of tour guide.

A: *And in the municipality of S up until 2001 when mayor A.L. arrives there was not—there was no tourism department either, was there?*

I: Y en el municipio de S hasta el 2001 en que llega el alcalde A.L.M. tampoco existía lo que se llama un departamento de turismo, ¿no es así?

W: Eso es correcto.

I: That's correct.

A: And Mr. A.L.M., uh, appointed some people, uh, created this department and appointed some people to this department?

[Objection]

A: *A.L.M., when he arrived in 2001, he, uh, created the office or the department of tourism separate from the department of public relations?*

I: ¿Y el alcalde A.L.M., a su llegada en el 2001, creó la oficina o el departamento de turismo en el municipio?

[Objection]

W: ¿Qué si A.L.M. creó un departamento de turismo?

I: Is the question whether *A.L.M.* created a tourism department?

W: Entiendo que sí.

I: That's—my understanding is that that's the case.

A: *¿Now, you also said that you had a computer at public relations?*

I: ¿También acierta usted que tenía una computadora en relaciones públicas?

W: Eso es correcto.

I: That's correct.

A: Was that computer on your desk?

I: ¿Esa computadora se hallaba en su escritorio?

W: Sí.

I: Yes.

A: *When you were appointed in 98 to your career position of typist clerk, that was also the time frame when you were appointed, uh, electoral commissioner?*

I: ¿Cuando usted la nombraron en el 98 a su puesto de carrera de mecanógrafa coincidió esa época con su nombramiento como comisionaria de escuela— comisionado electoral?

W: *Yo estuve trabajando en el municipio desde mucho antes de ser comisionada electoral—*

I: Well, I was working at the muni—municipality far before I was ever made electoral commissioner—

W: *—Y cuando estuve de comisionada electoral fue por corto periodo de tiempo porque pasó el huracán G y estuve en los refugios—*

I: And—

W: —Trabajando para el municipio—

I: And, uh, when I was named electoral commissioner I spent very little time in that position. Because when I was appointed to that position hurricane G came and I spent my time—and I spent time at the shelters helping out, uh, the muni—helping the municipality out.

A: *So when you say that you were appointed as electoral commissioner, commissioner in your direct, that was just for 2 or 3 months?*

I: ¿Entonces cuando usted dice que usted fue nombrada comisionada electoral, eh, en su testimonio en el directo, a caso eso fue únicamente por 2 ó 3 meses?

W: Sí.

I: Yes.

A: *Now, this computer that you had on your desk at public relations, uh, did you use it for, uh, uh, your work?*

I: Y bien, ¿esta computadora que usted tenía en su escritorio en relaciones públicas la usaba usted para su trabajo?

W: Para mi trabajo de relaciones públicas, objetivamente sí.

I: For my work in public relations, well objectively yes.

A: Does that computer have a program for the internet?

I: Esa computadora, ¿tiene un programa para la internet?

W: No. Esa no tenía internet.

I: No. That one didn't have internet.

A: The one that was on your desk didn't have it?

I: La que se en,

W: No.

I: No.

A: Did you use any other computer?

I: ¿Usó alguna otra computadora?

W: Luego llegó otra computadora que tenía acceso a la internet—

I: Afterwards—

W: —Y no—Y la usaba E.L.T. —

I: Afterwards another computer with access to the internet was brought in and it was used by E.L.T.

A: What was E.L.T.'s political affiliation?

I: ¿Cuál es la afiliación política? —

[Objection, irrelevant. Judge overruled]

I: ¿Cuál es la afiliación política de E.L.T.?

W: Según él me ha expresado, es X.

I: Well, according to what he has told me he is an X.

A: *And Mr. E.L. was the one that was—that had the position of administrative assistant, didn't he?*

I: Y E.L. era el que ocupaba el puesto de asistente administrativo, ¿no es así?

W: Eso es así.

I: That's right.

A: *But when M.C. used to go outside of the office instead of appointing him as acting director she appointed you?*

I: Pero entonces, ¿cuando M.C. salía de la oficina en lugar de nombrarlo a él como interino de la—como director la nombraba a usted?

W: Sí, pero eso tiene una explicación y lógica.

I: Yes, but that has an explanation and it's very logical.

W: *E. L. T., le digo yo siempre que es el compositor, es una persona—*

I: E. L. T., I would tell you he's a composer. He is a person that—

W: —Y tiene otras ta—y tiene ese tipo de tareas—

I: And he has those kinds of tasks—

W: *En el caso mío, tenía más conocimiento sobre el sistema de oficina y que se hacía en la oficina—*

I: In my case, I had greater knowledge as to the office system and what was carried out at, uh, the offi—what was done at the office—

W: —*Y por eso entiendo que entonces me dejaba a cargo a mí*—

I: And, so I understand that that's why she would leave me in charge—

W: —Y a él le gustaba estar allí transcribiendo, componiendo—

I: He would like to be over there writing his—composing his songs—

W: —No. No canciones. No. No. Escritos—

I: Drafting [unintelligible]—

W: —Haciendo trabajos de anuarios—

I: Uh, doing yearbook work—

W: —*Economizando en la oficina mucho dinero porque, este, se realizaban allí*—

I: Uh, saving a lot of money for the municipality, because the work was done there—

A: Would you go by his computer and see that he was doing that job?

I: ¿Pasaba usted por la computadora de él y lo veía a él haciendo ese tipo de trabajo?

W: *Sí. Él trabajaba en eso. No, o sea, no estaba en su computadora dibujando pero sí sabía lo que estaba haciendo.*

I: Yes. He works at that. Not that I would get into his computer to find out what he was doing. But yes, he was working on that.

A: *Now, as administrative office system, would you happen to know why at the public works—public relations' computers and particularly the programs on the internet there was electoral work there and signs regarding elections?*

[Objection]

I: Y bien, ¿como directora interina de la oficina de relaciones públicas tenía usted conocimiento de la razón por la cual, eh, había en esa computadora trabajo de índole electoral y los accesos de la internet, eh, se habían hecho accesos a puntos electorales?

W: Negativo. Ni siquiera entiendo lo que me está diciendo.

I: Negative. I don't even unde—I don't even get it—get what you're saying.

A: So you don't know?

I: ¿Entonces usted no sabe?

A: *Okay. Now, you were transferred on January 18th to emergencias médicas. Medical emergencies.*

I: Y entonces la trasladaron el 18 de enero para emergencias médicas.

A: *When you arrived there on January 18th at that moment this situation that you explained on the direct, there was no chair for you, the typewriter—there was no typewriter. The fax, computer, and photocopier were broken down. Did you find that when you arrived there?*

I: Cuando a usted la trasladan el 18 de enero a emergencias médicas, en ese momento la situación que usted describió que no había, eh, la situación que usted describió en su directo, en su interrogatorio directo, que indicó que no había ni silla ni maquinilla. Y que el fax y la copiadora estaban, eh, dañados.

A: *Was that situation—did you find that situation that day?*

I: Eh, ¿se enteró usted de esa situación en ese día?

W: Eso es correcto.

I: That's correct.

A: How many days had the new administration been there?

I: ¿Cuántos días llevaba la nueva administración ahí?

W: No sé—entraron el siete, pues 18, pues—

I: Well—

W: —14, 7, 8, 9, 10. 8, 9, 10 dias. No sé. Este—

I: Well, if they took office the 7th, uh, 14, 8, 9, 10. 10 days. I don't know.

A: *Now, isn't it true Mrs. D.S. that you took certain things to the office, because you were moving from your house and you didn't have space to have them.*

I: ¿No es cierto, Sra. D.S. que usted llevó ciertos artículos a su oficina porque usted se hallaba en el medio de una mudanza de su casa y no tenía espacio para tener esos artículos?

W: Bueno, yo llevo mi silla porque tengo que sentar—

I: Well, I took my chair because I needed to sit down somewhere—

W: —Llevo la maquinilla porque quiero hacer trabajos—

I: I take my typewriter, because I want to do work.

W: *Y llevo un escritorio porque mi compañera L.N.A. iba a llegar y no tenía donde sentarse.*

I: And I took my desk because my co-worker L.N.A. was coming and she didn't have a place to sit down.

W: *Yo podía fácilmente, no sé, dejarlo allí, porque la casa es de mi mamá, pues, este,*

I: I could have very well have left it there, because the house belongs to my mother.

W: Lo hice de buena voluntad. De buena fe.

I: I did it out of goodwill.

W: *Yo no llegué con una—una, o sea, yo no llegué de una manera hostil al departamento.*

I: I didn't—

W: —Yo llegué a trabajar.

I: I did not arrive at that department in a hostile fashion. I arrived there, eh, willing to work.

A: Mrs. D.S., were you moving?

I: Sra. D.S., ¿se mudaba usted?

W: Sí.

I: Yes.

A: *And at that place where you were moving there was no space for that desk, was there?*

I: Y al lugar donde se mudaba usted no había espacio para ese escritorio, ¿no es así?

W: Bueno, de haberlo—de haberlo lo podía haber.

I: Well, having—having space. There—there could have been space.

W: *Pero no un espacio donde se vea bonito. A lo mejor en la marquesina, pues.*

I: But perhaps not, uh, in a place—in a location where it would, uh, look nicely. Perhaps in the garage.

Bibliography

Alexieva, B. 1994. On teaching note-taking in consecutive interpreting. In *Teaching interpreting and translation II*, ed. C. Dollerup and A. Lindegaard, 1999–2006. Amsterdam: John Benjamins.

Atkinson, R. L., and R. M. Stiffrin. 1968. Human memory: A proposed system and its control processes. In *The psychology of learning and motivation*, ed. K. W. Spence and J. T. Spence. London: Academic Press.

Bailey, F. L., and H. B. Rothblatt. 1971. *Successful techniques for criminal trials*. New York: Lawyers Co-operative.

Baddeley, A. D. 1966. The influence of acoustic and semantic similarity on long-term memory for word sequences. *Quarterly Journal of Experimental Psychology* 18: 302–309.

———. 1992. *Human memory: Theory and practice*. Hove: Lawrence Erlbaum.

Baddeley, A. D., N. Thompson, and M. Buchanan. 1975. Word length and the structure on memory. *Journal of Verbal Learning and Verbal Behaviour* 1: 575–89.

Barik, H. C. 1973. Simultaneous interpretation: Temporal and quantitative data. *Language and Speech* 16: 237–70.

Benmaman, V. 2000. Interpreter issues on appeal. *Proteus: Newsletter of the National Association of Judicial Interpreters and Translators* 9: 1–13.

Berk-Seligson, S. 1988. The need for quality interpreting services in the courtroom. *The Courtroom Manager* 3: 10–14.

———. 1989a. The role of register in the bilingual courtroom: Evaluative reactions to interpreted testimony. *International Journal of the Sociology of Language* 79: 79–91.

———. 1989b. The impact of politeness in witness testimony: The influence of the court interpreter. *Multilingua* 7: 441–49.

———. 1999. The impact of court interpreting on the coerciveness of leading questions. *Forensic Linguistics* 6: 30–56.

———. 2002. *The bilingual courtroom: Court interpreters in the judicial process*. Chicago: University of Chicago Press.

Blackwell, S. 1996. Corrective measures: Some aspects of transcription in the British legal system. In *Recent developments in forensic linguistics*, ed. H. Kniffka, S. Blackwell and R. M Coulthard, 255–76. Frankfurt am Mein: Peter Lang.

Bouma, A. 1990. *Lateral asymmetries and hemispheric specialization: Theoretical models and research*. Amsterdam: Swets and Zeitlinger.

Brennan, S. E., and M. F. Schober, 2001. How listeners compensate for disfluencies in spontaneous speech. *Journal of Memory and Language* 44: 274–96.

Bridge, D. J., J. P. Provyn, Z. Yaofei, and M. W. Howard. 2006. Memory processes and gender influences: A matter of context, www.memory.syr.edu/papers/BridgeEtal-doc.pdf (accessed July 15, 2007).

Brown, P., and S. Levinson. 1978. Universals in language usage: Politeness phenomena. In *Questions and politeness: strategies in social interaction*, ed. E. Goody, 56–311 Cambridge: Cambridge University Press.

Bruning, J. L. and B. L. Kintz. 1987. *Computational handbook of statistics*. Glenview, Ill.: Scott, Foresman.

Buckner, J. P., and R. Fivush. 1998. Gender and self in children's autobiographical narratives. *Applied Cognitive Psychology* 12: 407–29.

Chambers, J. C. 1992. Linguistic correlates of gender and sex. *English World-Wide* 13: 173–218.

Christoffels, I. K., and A. M. B. De Groot. 2005. Simultaneous interpreting: A cognitive perspective. In *Handbook of bilingualism: Psycholinguistic approaches*, ed. J. F. Kroll and A. M. B. De Groot, 454–79. New York: Oxford University Press.

Colley, A., J. Bell, N. Kirby, R. Harvey, and I. Vingelem. 2002. Gender-linked differences in everyday memory performance: Effort makes the difference. *Sex Roles: A Journal of Research* 47: 577–82.

Conley, J. M., W. M. O'Barr, and E. A. Lind. 1978. The power of language: Presentational style in the courtroom. *Duke Law Journal* 78: 1375–99.

Conley, J. M., and W. M. O'Barr. 1998. *Just words: Law, language and power*. Chicago: University of Chicago Press.

Court interpreters feel impact of illegal immigration caseload. 2005. *Newsletter of the Federal Courts* 37, http://www.uscourts.gov/ttb/feb05ttb/interpreters/index.html (accessed February 6, 2006).

Crawford, M. and L. English. 1994. Generic versus specific inclusion of women in language: Effects on recall. *Journal of Psycholinguistic Research* 13: 373–81.

Dam, H. V. 2004. Interpreter's notes: On the choice of language. *Interpreting* 6: 3–17.

De Groot, A. M. B. 1997. The cognitive study of translation and interpretation: Three approaches. In *Cognitive processes in translation and interpreting*, ed. J. H. Danks, G. M. Shreve, S. B. Fountain, and M. K. McBeath, 25–56. Thousand Oaks, CA: Sage.

Eckert, P., and S. McConell-Ginet. 2003. *Language and gender*. Cambridge: Cambridge University Press.

Edwards, A. B. 1995. *The practice of court interpreting*. Amsterdam: John Benjamins.

Fabbro, F., and L. Gran. 1994. Neurologinal and neuropsychological aspects of polyglossia and simultaneous interpretation. In *Bridging the gap: Empirical research in simultaneous interpretation*, ed. S. Lambert and B. Moser-Mercer, 273–317. Amsterdam: John Benjamins.

Fraser, B. 1988. Types of English discourse markers. *Acta Linguistica Hungarica* 38: 19–33.

———. 1993. Discourse markers and second language learning. *Proceedings of the Pragmatics and Second Language Learning Conference*, Chicago: University of Illinois.

———. 1996. Pragmatic markers. *Pragmatics: International Pragmatics Association* 6: 167–90.

———. 2005. Whither politeness. In *Broadening the horizon of linguistic politeness*, ed. R. T. Lakoff and S. Ide, 65–82. Amsterdam: John Benjamins.

Friedman, A., and A. Pines. 1991. Sex differences in gender-related childhood memories. *Sex Roles* 25: 25–32.

Gerver, D. 1974. The effects of noise on the performance of simultaneous interpreters: Accuracy and performance. *Acta Psychologica* 38: 159–67.

———. 1976. Empirical studies of simultaneous interpretation: A review and a model. In *Translation: Applications and research*, ed. R. W. Briskin, 165–207. New York: Gardner. Gile, D., H. V. Dam, and A. Schjoldager. 2001. Introduction to *Getting started in interpreting research*, ed. D. Gile and H. V. Dam, vii–xiv. Amsterdam: John Benjamins.

Gile, D. 1990. *Basic concepts and models for conference interpretation training*. Paris: INALCO & CEEI (ISIT).

———. 1995. *Basic concepts and models for interpreter and translator training*. Amsterdam: John Benjamins.

Gillies, A. 2005. *Note-taking or consecutive interpreting: A short course*. Manchester: St. Jerome.

Goffman, E. 1956. *The presentation of self in everyday life*. New York: Doubleday.

Goldman-Eisler, F. 1972. Segmentation of input in simultaneous translation. *Journal of Psycholinguistic Research* 1: 127–40.

González, R., V. Vásquez, and H. Mikkelson. 1991. *Fundamentals of court interpretation: Theory, policy and practice*. Durham, NC: Carolina Academic Press.

Grice, H. P. 1975. Logic and conversation. In *Syntax and semantics 3: Speech acts*, ed. P. Cole and J. L. Morgan, 41–58. New York: Academic Press.

Grosjean, F. 1997. The bilingual individual. *Interpreting* 2: 163–87.

Hale, S. B. 1996a. Pragmatic considerations in court interpreting. *Australian Review of Applied Linguistics* 19: 61–72.

———. 1996b. You shall truly and faithfully interpret the evidence. What does this mean to the court interpreter. *XVI World Congress of the Fédération Internationales* 1: 424–31.

———. 1997a. The interpreter on trial: Pragmatics in court interpreting. In *The critical link: Interpreters in the community*. ed. S. E. Carr, R. Roberts, A. Dufour, and D. Steyn, 207– 11. Amsterdam: John Benjamins.

———. 1997b. Clash of world perspectives: The discursive practices of the law, the witness, and the interpreter. *Forensic linguistics: The International Journal of Speech, Language, and the Law* 4: 197–209.

———. 1997c. The treatment of register variation in court interpreting. *Translator: Studies in Intercultural Communication* 3: 39–54.

———. 2004. *The discourse of court interpreting*. Amsterdam: John Benjamins.

Hale, S. B., and J. Gibbons. 1999. Varying realities: Patterned changes in the interpreter's representation of courtroom and external realities. *Applied Linguistics* 20: 203–20.

Herlitz, A., F. Airaksinen, and E. Nordstrom. 1997. Sex differences in episodic memory: The impact of verbal and visuospatial ability. *Neuropsychology* 13: 590–7.

Herlitz, A., L. G. Nilsson, and L. Blaeckmann. 1997. Gender differences in episodic memory. *Memory and Cognition* 25: 801–11.

Holmes, J. 1995. *Women, men and politeness*. London: Longman.

Holmes, J. 1998. Women's talk: The question of sociolinguistic universals. In *Language and gender: A reader*, ed. J. Coates, 461–83. Malden, Massachusetts: Blackwell.

Hultsch, D. F., M. E. Masson, and B. J. Small. 1991. Adult age differences in direct and indirect tests of memory. *Journal of Gerontology: Psychological Sciences* 46: 22–30.

Isham, W. P. 1994. Memory for sentence form after simultaneous interpretation: Evidence both for and against deverbalization. In *Bridging the gap: Empirical research in simultaneous interpretation*, ed. S. Lambert and B. Moser-Mercer, 191–211. Amsterdam: John Benjamins.

———. 2000. Phonological interference in interpreters of spoken-languages: An issue of storage or process? In *Language processing and simultaneous interpreting*, ed. B. Englund Dimitrova and K. Hyltenstam, 133–49. Amsterdam: John Benjamins.

Isham, W. P., and H. Lane. 1994. A common conceptual code in bilinguals: Evidence from simultaneous interpreting. *Sign Language Studies* 85: 291–316.

Kade, O., and C. Cartellieri. 1971. Some methodological aspects of simultaneous interpreting. *Babel* 17: 12–16.

Kimura, D., and P. G. Clarke. 2003. Women's advantage on verbal memory is not restricted to concrete words. *Psychological Reports* 91: 1137–42.

Kennedy, P. 1994. *A guide to econometrics*. Cambridge, Mass.: MIT Press.

Lado, R., and E. Blansitt. 1967. *Contemporary Spanish*. New York: McGraw-Hill.

Lakoff, R. 1975. Language and woman's place. *Language in Society* 2: 45–160.

———. 2005. Introduction to *Language and women's place: Text and commentaries and expanded version*, ed. M. Bucholtz, 77–119. Oxford: Oxford University Press

Lakoff, R. T., and S. Ide. 2005. Introduction to *Broadening the horizon of linguistic politeness*, ed. R. T. Lakoff and S. Ide, 1–22. Amsterdam: John Benjamins.

Levelt, W. 1983. Monitoring and self-repair in speech. *Cognition* 14: 41–104.

Levelt, W. 1989. *Speaking: From intention to articulation*. Cambridge: MIT Press.

Linell, P., C. Wadenjö, and L. Jönsson. 1992. Establishing communicative contact through a dialogue interpreter. In *Communication for specific purposes*, ed. A. Grindsted and J. Wagner, 125–42. Tübingen: Gunter Narr.

Lind, E. A., and W. M. O'Barr. 1979. The social significance of speech in the courtroom. In *Language and social psychology*, ed. H. Giles and R. St. Clair, 66–87. College Park, MD: University Press.

London, H. 1973. *Psychology of the persuader*. Morristown, NJ: General Learning Press.

Lonsdale, D. 1997. Modeling cognition in SI: Methodological issues. *Interpreting* 2: 91–117.

MacKinnon, C. A. 1989. *Toward a feminist theory of the state*. Cambridge: Harvard University Press.

Maitland, S. B., A. Herlitz, L. Nyberg, and L. G. Nilsson. 2004. Selective sex differences in declarative memory. *Memory & Cognition* 32: 1160–9.

Mattei, E., and T. Roeper. 1985. *Understanding and producing speech*. New York: Universe Books.

Matyssek, H. 1989. *Handbuch der notizentechnik: Ein weg zur sprachunabhängigen notation*. Heidelberg: Groos.

McAllister, J., S. Cato-Symonds, and B. Johnson. 2006. ERP responses to disfluencies in spontaneous speech, http://odur.let.rug.nl/nbl/program/22.html (accessed February 2, 2006).

McElhaney, J. W. 1974. *Effective litigation – – –Trials, problems, and materials*. St. Paul, MN: West.

Meyers-Levy, J. 1989. Gender differences in information processing: A selectivity interpretation. In *Cognitive and affective responses to advertising*, ed. P. Cafferata and A. M. Tybout, 219–60. Ontario, Canada: Lexington.

———. 1994. Gender differences in cortical organization: Social and biochemical antecedents and advertising consequences. In *Attention, attitude, and affect in response to advertising*, ed. E. Clark, T. Brock, and D. Steward, 107–22. Hillsdale, NJ: Lawrence Erlbaum.

Mikkelson, H. 1989. Interpreter survey. *Polyglot* 19: 11.

———. 1993. Consecutive interpretation. *The Reflector* 6: 5–9.

———. 1998. Towards a redefinition of the role of the court interpreter. *Interpreting* 3: 21–45.

———. 1999. Verbatim interpretation: An oxymoron, http:/www.acebo.com/papers/verbatim.htm (accessed June 7, 2006).

Miller, G. 1956. The magic number seven, plus, or minus two: Some limits of our capacity for processing information. *Psychology Review* 63: 81–97.

Minder, C. 1989. Court interpreters: An undervalued judicial resource. *The advocate: Official publication of the Idaho State Bar* 41: 12–13.

Mitchell-Kernan, C. 1972. Signifying and marking: Two Afro-American speech acts. In *Directions in sociolinguistics: The ethnography of communication*, ed. J. J. Gumperz and D. Hymes, 161–79. New York: Hold, Rinehart, and Winston.

Morrill, A. E. 1971. *Trial diplomacy*. Chicago: Court Practice Institute.

Morris, R. 1995. The moral dilemmas of court interpreting. *The Translator* 1: 25–46.

Moser, B. 1978. Simultaneous interpretation: A hypothetical model and its practical application. In *Language, interpretation and communication*, ed. D. Gerver and H. Sinaiko, 353–68. New York: Plenum.

Moser-Mercer, B., A. Künzli, and M. Korac. 1998. Prolonged turns in interpreting: Effects on quality, physiological and psychological stress (Pilot study). *Interpreting* 3: 47.

Mujica, B. 1982. *Entrevista*. New York: Holt, Rinehart & Winston.

Niska, H. 1995. Just interpreting: Role conflicts and discourse types in court interpreting. In *Translation and the law*, ed. M. Morris. Amsterdam: John Benjamins.

O'Barr, W. 1982. *Linguistic evidence: Language, power, and strategy in the courtroom*. New York: Academic Press.

O'Barr, W., and B. K. Atkins. 1980. Women's language or powerless language? In *Women and language in literature and society*, ed. S. McConnell-Ginet, R. Borker, and N. Furman, 93–110. Praeger: New York.

O'Barr, W., and A. E. Lind. 1977. Ethnography and experimentation—Partners in legal research. In *Perspectives in law and psychology: Vol. 1. The criminal justice system*, ed. B. D. Sales, 181–207. New York: Plenum.

Palma, J. 1995. Textual density and the judiciary interpreter's performance. In *Translation and the law*, ed. M. Morris, 219–37. Amsterdam: John Benjamins.

Peterson, R. L., and M. J. Peterson. 1959. Short-term retention of individual items. *Journal of Experimental Psychology 58*: 193–8.

Posner, M.I., and S. W. Keele. 1967. Decay of visual information from a single letter. *Science 158*: 137–9.

Pousada, A. 1979. Interpreting for language minorities in the courts. *Georgetown University Round Table on Languages and Linguistics*: 186–208.

Pomerantz, A. 1975. Second assessments: A study of some features of agreements/disagreements. PhD diss., University of California, Irvine.

Ramsey, M. M. 1957. *A textbook of modern Spanish*. New York: Holt, Rinehart and Winston.

Repa, J. 1991. Training and certification of court interpreters in a multicultural society. *META* 36: 595–605.

Rigney, A. C. 1997. Use and interpretation of discourse markers in a bilingual courtroom. *American Translators Association Journal*: 117–129.

Roy, C. 1989. A sociolinguistic analysis of the interpreter's role in turn-taking in interpreted events. PhD diss., Georgetown University.

Sacks, H., E. Schegloff, and G. Jefferson. 1974. A simplest systematic for the organization of turn-taking in conversation. *Language* 50: 696–735.

Schiffrin, D. 1985. Conversational coherence: The role of well. *Language* 61: 640–67.

——. 1987. *Discourse markers*. Cambridge: Cambridge University Press, 1987.

Seco, M. 1996. *Gramática esencial de la lengua española*. Madrid: Espasa.

Seleskovitch, D. 1978. *Interpreting for international conferences*. Arlington, VA: Pen & Booth.

Shuy, R. W. 1998. What we do in English when we take notes: Evidence from a civil suit. *Studia Anglica Posnaniensia* 33: 353–63.

Storey, C. J. 1996. A tale of two transcripts. Paper presented at the *International Association of Forensic Phonetics Conference*, in Wiesbaden, Germany.

Smith, F. 1985. *Reading without nonsense*. New York: New York Teacher's College Press.

Smith, V. L. and H. H. Clark. 1993. On the course of answering questions. *Journal of Memory and Language* 32: 25–38.

Solé, Y. R., and C. A. Solé. 1977. *Modern Spanish syntax: A study in contrast*. Lexington, MA: D. C. Heath.

Soto, O. N. 1969. *Repaso de gramática*. New York: Harcourt, Brace and World.

Tallerman, M. 2005. *Understanding syntax*. Oxford: Arnold.

Tannen, D. 1990. *You just don't understand: Women and men in conversation*. New York: William Morrow.

Vidal, M. 1997. New study on fatigue confirms need for working in teams. *Proteus* 69: 1–6.

Wadenjö, C. 1992. *Interpreting as interaction: On dialogue-interpreting in immigration hearings and medical encounters*. Linkoping: Linkoping University.

Wilson, D. 1975. *Presuppositions and non-truth conditional semantics*. New York: Academic Press.

Yonker, J. E., E. Eriksson, L. G. Nilsson, and A. Herlitz. 2003. Sex differences in episodic memory: Minimal influence of estradiol. *Brain and Cognition* 52: 231–8.

Index

About the Author

Dr. Marianne Mason is an Assistant Professor of Modern Languages and Linguistics at the Georgia Institute of Technology. Her areas of expertise include forensic linguistics, discourse analysis, pragmatics, and translation theory. She has published in the fields of forensic linguistics and discourse analysis in the *Journal of Pragmatics, Police Quarterly, Pragmatics: Journal of the International Pragmatics Association*, and the *ATA Chronicle*.